The Power
Experience Heaven's Authority

Dr. Kelafo Collie, M.D.
Shallaywa Collie, MBA

Copyright©2020 Dr. Kelafo Z. Collie, M.D., Shallaywa Collie, MBA

The Power Experience Heaven's Authority

ISBN 978-1-7355413-6-5

All rights reserved. No part of this book may be reproduced or transmitted in any form or by any means without written permission.

www.kelafozcollie.com

www.shallaywa.com

Published by:
Majestic Priesthood Publication,
Freeport, Grand Bahama, Bahamas.
Email: mpppublications@gmail.com

1-242-727-2137

Printed in the United States of America

The Power

Experience Heaven's Authority

Contents

Preface viii
Introduction xii

Segment One
KINGDOM FOUNDATION RE-CAP ON THE KINGDOM — 1

Chapter 1: Power Belongs To God 2
Chapter 2: The Kingdom Of God 30
Chapter 3: We Have A Heavenly Father 37
Chapter 4: The Authority Of The Kingdom Citizens 47
Chapter 5: Papa's Prosperity Plan 55

Segment Two
RESURRECTION POWER — 68

Chapter 6: Power Of Resurrection 69
Chapter 7: The Resurrection And Demonstration Of Jesus' Kingdom Power 78
Chapter 8: The Blood Of Jesus: Why The Blood Of Jesus Is So Powerful 87

Chapter 9: Experiencing The Power Of God 126

Chapter 10: Miracles Of The Kingdom 133

Segment Three
DELIVERANCE   149

Chapter 11: The Foundation Of Deliverance 150

Chapter 12: Religion Versus The Kingdom Of Jesus
Christ 186

Chapter 13: The Kingdom Of God Versus The Kingdom
Of Darkness 197

Chapter 14: Disarming The Enemy 217

Chapter 15: The Strong Man And The Strong Powers In
Your Life 229

Chapter 16: The Strong Man & The Spirits More
Powerful Than Him 240

Segment Four
HEALING   250

Chapter 17: Jesus The Healer 251

Chapter 18: The Father Gives Zoë Life 266

Chapter 19: Health, Healing And Supernatural Healing
.... 292

Chapter 20: Ministering To The Sick 302

Segment Five
ACCESS THE POWER   312

Chapter 21: All These Shall Be Added 313
Chapter 22: The Prayer Of God 322
Chapter 23: Carrying The Fire And The Healing 327
Chapter 24: 10 Powerful Prayers To Bring Victory In
               Your Life 336

Preface

POWER

Power is a widely sourced virtue or factor by almost all; young, old, boys, girls, men, women, Pastors, Members, Presidents, Governors, Ministers and people of several and every categories. Everyone wants to be able to give certain orders, control certain things in certain places and at certain times. Everyone wants to be in charge.

It is however a saddening truth to know that only a few surely knows the true source of power, and how best to access it. Power could make or mar both the one executing and the person or persons on whom power is executed. Power is a virtuous, amazing and useful weapon, but when not well used or understood, could become a dangerously destroying instruments.

Types of Power

Over the years, several types of power had been explained by several scholars which really are true when brought to the real world. Different factors birth different influence people have on others, resulting to several types of power. Let's address a few of them in brief;

1. Legitimate Power: Legitimate power is given/bestowed upon an individual as a result of a position (official) that such person occupies. The moment such person, due to one thing or the other, stops being in that position, the effectiveness of this power stops as far as the person is concerned.

2. Expert Power: This is a kind of power one has and exhibits as a result of profound knowledge/vast knowledge about something.

3. Reward Power. It's power based on rewards, opportunities, financial benefits etc.

4. Coercive Power: This is forcefully getting everyone to do what you want them to do. The execution of this power is not merciful at all as it seeks its own satisfaction only.

5. Reference Power: Here, the people naturally reverence or regard a person and as a result, will desire to do what such reverenced person desired or institute. I want to do what he/she tells us to because I like him/her. Influence birthed from natural love for a person.

Having talked about types of powers as established by several scholars, it is important to note that there's ONE power that supersedes all others.

Before one can make a wise and effective use of power, one must have vast understanding of it.

Hence, the need to understand power, its source, its essence and how best to use it. Could there be more to power than all these, could there be a better power? We will know in no time and this book will introduce/ reintroduce to some and express power and its true source.

The Ultimate Power

As said earlier, there is ONE POWER that supersedes all others. For this power to be referred to as being final, then, it has to be above all others in all ramifications. When compared to legitimate power, which has time boundaries, it must live/exist beyond time (timeless-out of time). When compared with Reward Power, it must have an existence with our without reward, such that even if it gives rewards its reward is out of time, like forever! When compared to reference Power, it must be a sacred power such that its default state and nature is referenced, not waiting for reference from others, but in its own self is honor! When compared with coercive power, it should be able to influence others without any iota of threat or forcefulness. It is better by far in all ramifications! What power could this be then?

This power is usually revealed by those from the Kingdom of God where Jesus is King forever, amen. They exhibit this power based on the ability to understand that they are a part of the Kingdom of God, although they live in this world – on earth. People who are a part of this Kingdom are aware that their King lives on their inside. How could this be you may say? You will be able to understand that they don't look here and there for authority, their highest authority (the King) dwells within them.

Here, we speak of no other power, but, the Power of God, and as regards to those in this Kingdom, we speak of no other persons but the believers and those who honestly and earnestly desire the Kingdom, Power and Glory of God.

Introduction

The power of any being is the proof of that being's existence. Power as being defined scientifically, as the ability to do work. In other words, power is the ability to do.

In another perspective, power is the ability to get others to do. A powerful man, in terms of influence, is the one who has the capacity to make others get things done. When a man is powerful, he does not just have the capacity to do, he also has the capability to get others to do what he would have done, and what He intends to do.

In this piece, we shall be studying the dimensions of God's power. Be blessed as you read.

The power of God

The Power of God operate beyond boundaries, countries, cultures etc. This power is final and complete. It needs no addition or subtraction or goes by seasons. God, Elohim, exists because he existed and he exist and will exist. He is the source of power. By source, we mean origin. He is the author, the process and the finisher of this Power. In Him is this power perfected. To operate this power effectively, a vast knowledge of God is needed. It is important to note that this power of God explains the person of God.

How then is the power of God described and explained?

> .... it is the power of God that brings salvation to everyone who believes (Romans 1:16)

> ......unto us which are saved it is the power of God (1 Corinthians 1:18

> ....CHRIST the power of God, and the wisdom of God." (1 Corinthians 1:24)

1 Corinthians 1:24 out rightly tells us that the power of God is in the person of Christ. I should reiterate that the power of God is expressly in the person of Christ Jesus.

Who then is Christ Jesus?

Who is Christ Jesus? The Bible says, "In the Beginning GOD created the heaven and the earth" (GENESIS 1:1)

The 'God' in this text has been proven over time by Bible scholars to mean 'Elohim' in Hebrew and the word 'Elohim' is used to mean 'Gods' or 'deities'. This is not to say the Almighty is more than one or to separate the trinity, but rather, to make us understand that the trinity is three persons in one being! Same being with different offices.

When Gen1:1 is compared with John1:1-5 which says

> "In the beginning was the word, and the word was with God, and the word was God. The same was in the beginning with God. All things were made by Him; without Him was not anything made that was made. In Him was life; and the life was the light of men. And the light shineth in darkness; and the darkness comprehended it not." (John 1:1-5 KJV)

From John, we understand that the Word created all things, and a careful look into the pronoun "HIM' used makes us understand that the Word is a personality. Vs14 further clears our doubt

> **JOHN 1:14** And the Word was made flesh, and dwelt among us, (and we beheld his glory, the glory as of the only begotten of the Father,) full of grace and truth.

Making us understand that this person of the Word became flesh and dwelt among is. All these are found in the person of Christ Jesus who was made a little lower than even the angels He created (Heb2:7, 9). He came into the world to achieve an ETERNAL purpose. Hence,

Christ Jesus usually referred to as "Second in God-head" by Christians not to belittle his personality, or make one in the God-head supreme than the other, (because the trinity is one), but rather, to say He is the second in office, not Being– Being is ONE in this regard!

Why then will God ever make Himself a little lower than creatures made by Him? Why would He want to do that?

The answer to this is found in John3:16

"For God so loved the world that he gave his only begotten son, that whosoever believeth in him should not perish, but have everlasting life."

Love! Love!! Love!!! This is the only reason He did. All Christ did, He did for Love. The uppermost in His heart while He did all He did was Love for me, you and everyone else.

What He did

Isa 53:3-5 "He is despised and rejected of men; a man of sorrows, and acquainted with grief: and we hid as it were our faces from him; he was despised, and we esteemed him not. Surely he hath borne our griefs, and carried our sorrows: yet we did esteem him stricken, smitten of God, and afflicted. But he was wounded for our transgressions, he was bruised for our iniquities: the chastisement of our peace was upon him; and with his stripes we are healed."

He became flesh, came into the world to bore the sin of the world.

> "For he hath made him to be sin for us, who knew no sin; that we might be made the righteousness of God in him."
> 2 Corinthians 5:21

He became sin so through Him, we are made God's righteousness in Him. He became curse for our sakes that we may live above the curse of the law. He died for our sins, according to the scriptures, was buried and rose for our justification. (Romans 4:25)

The summary of the LOVE OF GOD is in all that Christ did, in that He was made a sacrificial lamb, so by way of His sacrifice, we are made right with the Father.

Segment One

Kingdom Foundation
Re-Cap on the Kingdom

Chapter One

Power Belongs To God

Power is something lots of people desire. People desire power and the ability to accomplish the things that they want to accomplish. Men would go to any length so as to get power. Most people want to wedge a level of authority and control over certain of people.

What is Power that men could go to any length to get it? Power is possession of control, authority, or influence over things or people. It's also the ability to act or produce an effect.

Everything we see today on earth, the weather seasons, etc. should not be viewed without emphasizing on the immense power of God, the creator of Heavens and the Earth!

> God has spoken once, twice have I heard this: that power belongs to God. Psalm 62:11

God existed and is still existing in power. The systems of the world is coordinated by His power.

God is the source of power but it's quite unfortunate that the fundamental essence of power was abused by the influence of the devil. That's why it is so obvious today that evil powers are contending with the power of the Lord.

If God hath spoken once; nothing more is necessary! Heaven and earth shall pass away, but His word abides forever. How befitting His divine majesty!

We poor mortals may speak often and yet fail to be heard. He speaks but once and the thunder of His power is heard on a thousand hills.

When we talk about the power of God, which is the true power most are looking for but are not looking at the right place, "True power, which is the ability to exercise authority effectively, belongs to God alone and can only be found in Him" In scripture, the only true strength is the omnipotent sovereignty exercised by God, or ability that finds its source in God. No one has power unless God allows it. Jesus Christ through his sacrifice has been given of this power, and members of the body of Christ do too.

In the Old Testament, power and might are attributed above all to God. His power is shown both in the fact that He created the world, and that He sustains it as well; and He remains more powerful than all the forces within it.

His power is also seen in His mighty acts of salvation which, of course, is the most important power to us.

When God delegates His authority to human beings there is a certain power that it provides. And so, mankind has a great deal of God-given power over the earth to care for and properly use it.

> **Genesis 1:26-28** Then God said, "Let Us make man in Our image, according to Our likeness; let them have dominion [authority, power] over the fish of the sea, over the birds of the air, and over the cattle, over all the earth and over every creeping thing that creeps on the earth." So God created man in His own image; in the image of God He created him; male and female He created them. Then God blessed them, and God said to them, "Be fruitful and multiply; fill the earth and subdue it; have dominion over the fish of the sea, over the birds of the air, and over every living thing that moves on the earth."

Although God has given limited authority and power to mankind, He still often actively intervenes showing His power in miraculous works, especially of deliverance. It was with a "mighty hand and outstretched arm" that He brought His people out of Egypt and demonstrated His power in giving them the Promised Land.

As we see in the New Testament, the emphasis of God's use of His power shifts more to the spiritual. Christ had all authority given him by His Father, and He used it to forgive sins, and to cast out evil spirits. He gives authority to His disciples to become sons of God and to share in His work. God's power is constantly flowing.

The greatest show of His power of deliverance is in the area of our individual calling and conversion to His truth, to His way of life. Just before His ascension to heaven, Christ told the apostles,

> "Behold, I send the Promise of My Father upon you; but tarry in the city of Jerusalem until you are endued with power from on high." Luke 24:46

This was to happen on the Day of Pentecost, when the power of God's Spirit would become operative in the life of the church. Even after the great demonstration of God's powerful Holy Spirit on that first Pentecost of the first church era, the Apostle Paul found it necessary to encourage the Church with regard to the "exceeding greatness of God's power."

He prayed for knowledge to be given to the Ephesian members so they could know the power of God that was already working in them. He wanted to assure them that true Christians can always be confident in God's promises.

> "the eyes of your understanding being enlightened; that you may know what is the hope of His calling, what are the riches of the glory of His inheritance in the saints, and what is the exceeding greatness of His power toward us who believe, according to the working of His mighty power which He worked in Christ when He raised Him from the dead and seated Him at His right hand in the heavenly places, far above all principality and power and might and dominion, and every name that is named, not only in this age but also in that which is to come. And He put all things under His feet, and gave Him to be head over all things to the Church, which is His body, the fullness of Him who fills all in all." Ephesians 1:18-23

Apostle Paul looks back to the resurrection as the primary evidence of God's power, and sees the Gospel as the means by which that power comes to work in people's lives.

> "Romans 1:16 For I am not ashamed of the Gospel of Christ, for it is the power of God to salvation for everyone who believes [or has faith], for the Jew first and also for the Greek."

In Ephesians 1, Apostle Paul is emphasizing the power of God in the saints, rather than the power which God gives the saints. It is important to realize that this letter to the Ephesians does not say that salvation is the result of something we do, plus the power that is given to us by God. It is not a matter of "I plus the power of God." Salvation is the result of God's power at work—in us and through us.

Verse 19 tells us, ". . . what is the immeasurable greatness of His power in us who believe." Apostle Paul is emphasizing the power of God in us. Of course, it is true to say that God gives us strength and power; and we need that power constantly. But the scripture says that God's power resides in us.

Apostle Paul is trying to make us to see and realize—that the greatness of God's power is in us, what He is doing is in us. The result should be that our fears vanish, and we should have a new confidence and assurance with respect to our salvation.

Apostle Paul is very clear in his letter about the nature of the call itself and how it is founded on the character of God. He gives us a glimpse into the glory for which we are destined. And then, in verse 19, he emphasizes the power of God working in us.

He is very concerned about the Ephesian members (and us as well). He knows that they have believed, that they have trusted in Jesus Christ, and that they have been sealed by the Holy Spirit. Even still, he is praying for them without ceasing, and praying that they will advance into greater knowledge and understanding of what God is working out in us, and the potential that that opens up.

When we consider our frail bodies we know that they are susceptible to illnesses, and we find it almost impossible to believe, or even to imagine, that we could enjoy a state of glory.

And then, added to this, there is life as we know it in this world, with its changing circumstances. There is the world and its influence, friends, and others enticing us and tempting us to pursue earthly lusts. There is a preoccupation with worldly things, business affairs, and the need to make a living in order to maintain ourselves and our families. The list of distractions that we have is unlimited. All these things, the pressures of life and of circumstances, conspire together to make it seem impossible for us to find time for preparation for this glory.

Moreover, behind it all, we know that we are confronted by a powerful adversary, a subtle spiritual enemy, "as a roaring lion roaming about seeking whom he may devour, "confronting us at every weakness and who in his subtlety is constantly enticing, attracting and luring us into sin, failure and lethargy.

In addition, we realize that between us and that glory lies the fact of death (the last enemy) and the power of death and the grave.

These are the thoughts that can crowd into our minds, and they come especially to those who see most clearly "the riches of the glory of his inheritance in the saints. "Many know that God is great and powerful, but do not have a clue as to how He is going to do that. Many have an inkling, but we do not have a true vision or picture of it.

The power of God is that ability and strength whereby He can bring to pass whatsoever He pleases, whatsoever His infinite wisdom may direct, and whatsoever the infinite purity of His will may resolve . . . As holiness is the beauty of all God's attributes, so power is that which gives life and action to all the perfections of the Divine nature. How vain would be the eternal counsels, if power did not step in to execute them.

Without power His mercy would be but feeble pity. His promises an empty sound, His threatening a mere scare-crow. God's power is like Himself: infinite, eternal, incomprehensible; it can neither be checked, restrained, nor frustrated by the creature.

> The LORD also thundered in the heavens, and the Highest gave his voice; hailstones and coals of fire. Yea, he sent out his arrows, and scattered them; and he shot out lightening, and discomfited them. Then the channels of waters were seen and the foundations of the world were discovered at thy rebuke, O LORD, at the blast of the breath of thy nostrils" (Psa. 18:13-15).

> *Without power His mercy would be but feeble pity.*

God proportions His power to the nature of His work. The casting out of demons is ascribed to His "finger" (Luke 11:20); His delivering of Israel from Egypt to His "hand" (Exod. 13:9); but when the Lord saves a sinner, it is His "holy arm" which gets Him the victory (Psa. 98:1). It is to be duly noted that the language of Ephesians 1:19 is so couched as to take in the whole work of divine grace in and upon the elect. It is not restrained to the past—"who have believed according to," nor to the time to come—"the power that shall work in you." But, instead, it is "the exceeding greatness of his power to us-ward who believe." It is the "effectual working" of God's might from the first moment of illumination and conviction till their sanctification and glorification.

So dense is the darkness which has now fallen upon the people (Isa. 60:2), that the vast majority of those even in the "churches" deem it by no means a hard thing to become a Christian.

They seem to think it is almost as easy to purify a man's heart (James 4:8) as it is to wash his hands. That it is as simple a matter to admit the light of divine truth into the soul as it is the morning sun into our chambers by opening the shutters. That it is no more difficult to turn the heart from evil to good, from the world to God, from sin to Christ, than to turn a ship around by the help of the helm. And this, in the face of Christ's emphatic statement, "With men this is impossible" (Matt. 19:26).

To mortify the lusts of the flesh (Col. 3;5), to be crucified daily to sin (Luke 9:23), to be meek and gentle, patient and kind—in a word, to be Christ-like—is a task altogether beyond our powers. It is one on which we would never venture, or, having ventured on, would soon abandon, but that God is pleased to perfect His strength in our weakness, and is "mighty to save" (Isa. 63:1). It is only by His grace we are perfected and made righteous through Jesus Christ.

The POWER!

The Power of God as seen earlier is in the person of Christ. The person of Christ is summarized in that He died for us; Dying on the cross for our sins and rising for our justification. All that He did makes up the term 'GOSPEL' (1cor15:3, 4).

Paul in Romans 1:16 referred to this term 'GOSPEL' as the power of God.

> "For I am not ashamed of the Gospel of Christ: for it is the Power of God unto salvation to everyone that believeth; to the Jew first, and also to the Greek." Romans 1:16

If the Gospel then is the Power of God, how can one enjoy and operate in this power of God, remember, the

Kingdom is God's, the Power is God's, The Glory is God's and to exhibit power, there as to be ABILITY. Hence, what gives the ability to experience this Power that is of God?

> "That if thou shalt confess with thy mouth the Lord Jesus, and shalt believe in thine heart that God hath raised him from the dead, thou shalt be saved. For with the heart man believeth unto righteousness; and with the mouth confession is made unto salvation." Romans 10:9-10

From the text above, we see that the ability needed to operate in God's power very simple. God made it that simple in Christ Jesus. This ability is simply believing. John3:16 has a lot to say about this. It's indeed a popular text, but understood by a very few.

> "For God so loved the world that he gave his only begotten Son, that whosoever believeth in him should not perish, but have everlasting life." John 3:16

Wow, God loves the world! The knowledge of sin separated us from Him making us hide our faces from Him, but while we were yet in our hideouts (forgetting He's God over all seeing both the secret and the open) He kept loving us and desiring that we live before Him in freedom. As a result, He gave the only Son (in the person of Jesus) to become the sacrifice of reconciliation that through believing, other sons are birthed.

The only channel to operating in God's power is 'Believe', not through good deeds, self-righteousness, among others. But rather, through believing and believing alone. Who then can have this ultimate power of God? Remember where we started from, the legitimate power is enjoyed as a result of the office/position a person occupies, Reward is because others enjoy benefits from one etc. Every type of power has its specifications of who can and cannot own or have it. What then is the specification of this Kingdom Power?

The word "whosoever" from John 3:16 is the simplest answer to the question. This tells us that the power is not for some class of people but for everyone who has the needed ability, hence, power is for whosoever believes.

The Kingdom Power as earlier learnt is revealed in the person of Jesus Christ (1cor1:24), whosoever believes in the person of Christ and His sacrifice for the world has the ability needed to operate in Kingdom power.

The sacrifice of Christ is for the world! The King's Power is also a global thing meant for the world. People who are a part of the Kingdom of God, (those who have believed) can have this power bestowed upon them. They can even call forth things seen from things not seen, for example. Nations are blessed because of these people, generations are affected by these persons, their effects on generations are always positive because they source their power from the eternal source. This power has the ability to effect generations yet unborn because the author and the holder of this source lives out of time.

It pays

What Jesus did on the cross and the Heavenly Father's redemption plan to restore what has been lost to mankind gives us access to unlimited things through the power of the Holy Spirit. The Holy Spirit through His power gives us the Gifts and Fruits that we may have the wisdom and conduct to operate in all good things and prosper by the grace of God.

Fruit of the Spirit (Galatians 5-22-23)

- love,
- joy,
- peace,
- patience,
- kindness,
- goodness,
- faithfulness,
- gentleness, and
- Self-control.

Gifts of the Spirit (1 Corinthians 12:8–10)

- Word of wisdom

- Word of knowledge
- Faith
- Gifts of healings
- Miracles
- Prophecy
- Distinguishing between spirits
- Tongues
- Interpretation of tongues

Because of the power of Christ- he having rose from the dead and lives eternally as king. Receiving Christ as King and Lord makes us relevant to God forever! Forever isn't limited to life on Earth, no, but instead, even after death to this physical body, we will remain relevant to God.

This power gives us access to God both now and in eternity. It comes with several packages; from having all power and authority over the enemy (Luke 10:19) to understanding the mind of God.

Have you ever longed to be relevant, impactful or remembered positively, have you ever wanted fame, have you ever wanted to be a good leader? The only power that gives us access to all you desire is the power acquired from the Kingdom of God!

This power can be belittled or deprived of its maximum effectiveness where there is no understanding of its capacity and worth. It is therefore important that we look into the manual on which this power is written to understand the versatility of the power. The manual is no other but the HOLY BIBLE. The center message of the Bible is this King, and the King's Kingdom, Power and Glory.

THE AWESOME POWER OF GOD

In Exodus 8: 1-5,16-18, 20,21,24 we read of what God did and He did all these things through His finger. God is Spirit. He Word uses a language we can understand. A person cannot be in three places at once but God is not like that. The finger is only a small member of the body. Do you see how great God is? He did all these wonders only using His little finger. The river turned to blood; there were insects everywhere and He didn't have to exert Himself. Moses was given two tablets of stone written on by the finger of God. For the first time in history God wrote something for men that they could understand. God in heaven wrote a letter for people to keep. Moses and Aaron went to Pharaoh and asked him to let the Israelites go so that they could go and worship God. Moses was the first person to perform miracles. Why did God do this? It was so that Pharaoh would know that God exists. Moses took his staff and the dust became gnats that stung the people and animals. The river turned to blood. Pharaoh's magicians also turned the river into blood but then they could not turn it back into water again. Pharaoh's magicians could do some signs but when they made their sticks into snakes, Moses' snake swallowed their snakes. The power of God was much greater than their power.

The power of the Lord is as beautiful as the Lord's nature. The mind behind His power is not for destruction but to prove His love for mankind and that's what makes His power exceptional. The whole word recognizes that no other being or entity can compete with the power of the Lord. The universe continues to function according to design. We know upon what day the shortest day of the year will occur, and the longest. We know when the next solar eclipse will take place, how complete it will be, and from where it will be visible. And we expect to see both rain and sunshine in the coming days; seasons giving way to years.

What causes the world to be as it is? Many explanations have been offered by mankind; and many discarded. Some of these explanations are found in the myth and superstition of man. Ancient civilizations of both hemispheres; the Babylonians, Egyptians, Aztecs and Mayans. More recently, some have sought the answer by purely natural means. The shortcoming of these explanations is that, while they work reasonably well up to a point, they can never really explain how things began from nothing.

Then, there is the supernatural/natural explanation. This view holds that God created matter and the natural laws by which it is governed, The universe continues to operate according to His grand design in a natural way (Psalm 104:10-14;18,19; 24-25; 30).

As a believer in God, I believe that this latter explanation best answers the questions of origins. God is the cause of these things, they are the mysteries behind His awesomeness and they are working as they do so that our world is as it is (Matthew 5:45; Colossians 1:16, 17; Hebrews 1:2-3).

Noah's Ark

> "...and only Noah was left, together with those that were with him on the ark." (Genesis 7:23b; cf. vs 17-22).

God's judgement came upon the ancient world for its evil. Noah found favor in the eyes of God, and obeyed Him when instructed to do a strange thing; build a boat. He was mocked and ridiculed by many who ignored his pleas for them to repent. Only when the water began to rise and lift up the huge ark did they begin to wish they had Noah's boat-building ability. If this is so, then they still would miss the mark. This is because it was not Noah's boat-building ability that saved him. It was God's power. God's power saved Moses because Moses had obeyed God, putting his faith and trust in Him. Without this obedience, Noah would have perished along with the others, but still the source of Noah's salvation was not Noah, but God.

Moses' Staff

> "And as for you, lift up your staff and stretch out your hand over the sea and divide it, and the sons of Israel shall go through the midst of the sea on dry land." (Exodus 14:16; 15-28).

This is because the power was not in the staff, nor in Moses. The power was God's. The staff merely had a role to play in meeting God's condition for the releasing of His power.

The Bronze Serpent

> "Then the LORD said to Moses, 'Make a fiery serpent, and set it on a standard; and it shall come about that everyone, when he is bitten, when he looks at it he shall live." (Numbers 21:8; 5-9).

Of course, this was not some sort of medical breakthrough. The power was not in the serpent of molten brass, but in God. Centuries later, people would idolize the serpent, looking upon it as some sort of magical item (1 Kings 18:1-6). It was not. But people do similar things today with objects they esteem to be special.

The Ark of the Covenant

> "...let us take the ark of the covenant of the LORD that it may come among us and deliver us from the power of our enemies." (1 Samuel 4:3b; 1-4).

The Israelites during this period of their history were not being very true to the Law of God. But they did think the Ark of the Covenant, made 400 years before, contained some mystical power that would help them defeat their enemies if they took it to battle with them. Faithful living before God would have been much more beneficial to them. The power was in God; not in the ark. Of course, failing to realize this, they lost the battle.

The Jordan River

> "So he went down and dipped himself seven times in the Jordan, according to the word of the man of God; and his flesh was restored like the flesh of a little child, and he was clean." (2 Kings 5:14; cf. vss. 9-14).

Naaman was healed of his leprosy, but not by the power in the waters of the Jordan. It was God's power that had healed Naaman when he had placed his confidence in the word of the Lord by obeying.

Baptism

The point of the above examples is the same. Today, with respect to salvation, the power to save is God's. He does so in His own way, according to His own purpose. The power is not in the water of baptism, nor in our efforts to be baptized. But baptism is still the condition God has appointed which, when we meet it, His power will wash our sins away. Just as certainly has Noah had to build an Ark, or Naaman had to dip seven times, we must be baptized (Mark 16:16; Acts 2:38; Galatians 3:27; Colossians 2:12).

> *The source of Noah's salvation was not Noah, but God.*

In obeying the gospel, we are not showing confidence in ourselves or our works, but in God and His power to save us (1 Peter 3:20, 21; Romans 6:3, 4). In Psalm 8 verse 3 and 4, it says that God created the heavens and earth just with His finger. Only a few of the stars are visible. The light of some stars has not yet reached earth. What is son of man that you care for him?

Heathen's often recognize the power of God better than Christians do. Lukewarm Christians compromise and fail to discern good and evil. God's power is incomparably great and God manifested His power in delivering the people from Egypt. Some examples are through the miracles that Moses did and then when Jesus did miracles and drove out demons, the power of God was manifested. (Ephesians 1vesus 15). By the mighty power of God, Jesus was raised from the dead and Satan was placed under His feet. No matter who the demon is, or whether it is cancer of HIV, Jesus' name is greater than that. This power will cause you to be a victor in this world. A parent is afraid for his child because he doesn't know the power of God. He gives power over fear. Paul prayed for the Christians that their eyes would be enlightened. The three young men in the furnace of fire, in the book of Daniel knew the power of God.

In Ephesians 1, Apostle Paul deals with our problems and our difficulties. He prays that we may know "the exceeding greatness of His power toward us who believe, according to the working of His mighty power, which He worked in Christ when He raised Him from the dead and seated Him at His right hand in the heavenly places."

We will look at two main principles that Paul emphasizes here in Ephesians 1.

1. The greatness of the power in and of itself.
2. How we can be sure that this great power is working in us.

The greatness of the power in and of itself.

The process of Christian conversion and ultimate salvation is a demonstration of the power of God in us,

> "For I am not ashamed of the gospel, because it is the power of God that brings salvation to everyone who believes: first to the Jew, then to the Gentile." Romans 1:16

The eventual trouble with those who spend so much of their Christian lives in "the shadows and miseries" of doubt and vagueness and hesitancy, is that they have never really understood this first essential principle –No human can make himself a Christian; God alone makes Christians. Let us consider several supporting statements in Apostle Paul's epistles that show this spiritual power in us.

> "For Jews request a sign, and Greeks seek after wisdom; but we preach Christ crucified, to the Jews a stumbling block and to the Greeks foolishness, but to those who are called, both Jews and Greeks, Christ the power of God and the wisdom of God." I Corinthians 1:22-24

It was not on human terms and initiative by seeking a sign or wisdom, but on God's terms that man found what he needed; the power of God and the wisdom of God. In the preaching of Christ crucified, God called people by opening their eyes of faith to believe the gospel. That is the first step to seeing and believing God's power.

In Paul's eyes, preaching is of no value unless it is in "demonstration of the Spirit and of power."

> "For our gospel did not come to you in word only, but also in power, and in the Holy Spirit and in much assurance, as you know what kind of men, we were among you for your sake. And you became followers of us and of the Lord, having received the word in much affliction, with joy of the Holy Spirit." I Thessalonians 1:5-6

The response of the Thessalonian converts was a supernatural work of God, not a natural response to a clearly delivered sermon. When Apostle Paul preached to them, he did not just share human opinion and philosophy. Rather, his message was discernible by the power of God. The Holy Spirit brought it into their hearts with deep conviction. It is not by eloquence of words, or by the philosophy of human reasoning that we receive the message, but by the Spirit– the inspiration and the power of God that opens those things to our minds. Paul also tells us that Christians are God's workmanship.

> "For we are His workmanship, created in Christ Jesus for good works, which God prepared beforehand that we should walk in them." Ephesians 2:10

This truth is fundamental to an understanding of the Christian. Again, in writing to the Philippians, Apostle Paul says "being confident of this very thing, that He who has begun a good work in you will complete it until the day of Jesus Christ," in Philippians 1:6

This is God's power at work.

Again, in the same epistle we find:

> "For it is God who works in you both to will and to do for His good pleasure." Philippians 2:13

Also referring to his own preaching, Apostle Paul tells the Colossian members:

> To this end, I also labour, striving according to His working which works in me mightily. Colossians 1:29

Apostle Paul is speaking of the power of God working in him. He did not want the saints remaining spiritual babies; he wanted them to become spiritually mature. Elsewhere he prayed for complete sanctification of the saints. Paul preached the "fullness" of the gospel so that they could have the fullness of life that Jesus promised them. Apostle Paul expended all his God-given strength for this purpose. Developing maturity in the church members took a lot of work which was extremely tiring.

He gives power over fear.

He struggled and agonized like an athlete in an arena would. The power for this struggle came from God through Christ by the indwelling of the Holy Spirit.

Apostle Paul explains that what makes us Christian is that we are a new creation. We are not a remake; we are a new creation. We are nothing less than that. We are not merely a member of a church, we are not merely good people, and we are not merely people who have made a decision to become a member of God's church. A person can do all that, and still not be a true Christian.

When we are called, we have our responsibility to obey and overcome, but the entire teaching of the New Testament emphasizes above all else that we can do nothing until God has first done something in us. We are all spiritually dead by nature, and nobody can do anything until he has been given life and created new. And so, we are regenerated with new life. The power of God is the beginning and the end of salvation; everything is of Him and of His power.

How can we be sure that this great power is working in us?

In describing the power of God, Apostle Paul seems to struggle with human language to describe the power God uses. It will always be totally inadequate, but he tries.

> "....and what is the exceeding greatness of His power toward us who believe, according to the working of His mighty power." Ephesians 1:19

He prays here, that the Ephesians will know what is the "exceeding greatness"—not only the greatness, but the exceeding greatness. The word used by Apostle Paul that is translated into English as "exceeding" can also be translated "surpassing." God's power not only surpasses our power of expression, it surpasses our power of comprehension! For example, take all the dictionaries of the world, exhaust all the vocabularies, and when you have added them all together, you still have not begun to describe the greatness of God's power. There are no human words to describe it. Apostle Paul uses the best terms available, the surpassing greatness, the "exceeding greatness, "but they are not a sufficient description, so he adds to them by saying, "according to the working of His mighty power."

Let us analyze this new phrase, because it is one of the greatest that Apostle Paul uses.

We have to know "the exceeding greatness of His power toward us who believe, according to the working of His mighty power." A better word than "working "would be "vigor. Vigor is a much stronger word because it gives the impression of something that is effective or valuable and successful. Then take this second word "mighty "which stands for "strength"—strength in a very special way. Apostle Paul's word suggests a strength that overcomes, that prevails, that conquers, a strength that when it comes up against resistance, overcomes it. It is the kind of strength that can take down every high mountain, or it can raise every valley; there is nothing that can resist it. He is describing this power of God as "the dynamism of the strength" of the God to whom nothing is impossible.

In the New King James Version and King James Version as "power "really stands for "might"—the might of God, God's own essential might and inherent power. Apostle Paul is not using words here in a haphazard manner; there is a definite gradation in their use.

A similar glimpse of God's power is given by Isaiah in his prophecy. He expresses it by asking a series of rhetorical questions:

To whom can we liken God?

With whom can we compare Him? Once that is said, all comparisons are useless.

> It is He who sits above the circle of the earth, and its inhabitants are like grasshoppers, who stretches out the heavens like a curtain, and spreads them out like a tent to dwell in. Isaiah 40:22

No idols, political or governmental powers, presidents, prime ministers or governors, scholars or philosophers of wisdom in this world; nothing can compare with God's power. No one is able to advise Him or give Him anything; He is everything in and of Himself; He is everlasting in might and strength and power.

So, why do we doubt Him? Because we are human and we still have a great deal of human nature in us.

Chapter Reflections

1. _____

_____

2. _____

_____

3. _____

_____

Chapter Two

The Kingdom Of God

> "Jesus answered, Verily, verily, I say unto thee, except a man be born of water and *of* the Spirit, he cannot enter into the kingdom of God." - John 3:5

Most Believers are excited to hear about the Kingdom of God and the Kingdom of Heaven. They want to know how to access such a kingdom and some even want to abide there forever, just there.

But we must understanding of the Kingdom of God and the Kingdom of Heaven. What is common to everyone is that they mistake the Kingdom of God with the Kingdom of Heaven. The Kingdom of Heaven is used largely in the Book of Matthew Versus the Kingdom of God. It is thought this was to be sensitive to Jews who are accustomed to not say the Holy name of God, respecting its readers.

The Kingdom of God and the Kingdom of Heaven expresses the sovereignty of our Lord, King and ruler. It expresses the glory, beauty and holiness of our Lord. God is in control in this Kingdom.

In the four books of the Gospel, we can see that the Kingdom of God and Kingdom of Heaven are used interchangeably. This doesn't mean that the Kingdom of God and the Kingdom of Heaven are the same things. Even though they have some similarities, which include that they both are pure, they are filled with glory, they are controlled by God, and they involve the Trinity – they are two different things.

Life requires some basic things for those psychological needs– we need to eat, we need money, we need to get shelter, and we need clothes to put on – all these things are the main reason why men worry. The Lord said it himself. To get them is not easy, there are hurdles, and there are works that must be done. These things are the reason why we could read what Jesus said about the Kingdom of God.

> "But seek ye first the kingdom of God, and his righteousness; and all these things shall be added unto you." Matthew 6:33

What is the Kingdom of God? An explanation that was given about the Kingdom of God by Jesus ; "**But if I cast out devils by the Spirit of God, then the Kingdom of God is come unto you.**" Matthew 12:28

This is a hint to what the Kingdom of God is all about. The Kingdom of God is a Kingdom of holiness and purity. It is not a kingdom that demons (darkness and demonic forces) can stay. We can also say it is the Kingdom of Light.

> "And when he was demanded of the Pharisees, when the kingdom of God should come, he answered them and said, The Kingdom of God cometh not with observation: Neither shall they say, lo here! Or, lo there! For, behold, the Kingdom of God is within you." Luke 17:20-21

This again indicates that the Kingdom of God is a Kingdom that's already in the midst of man. It has been made available to man. This Kingdom indicates Jesus bringing the Holiness of God and the righteousness of God.

> "For the Kingdom of God is not meat and drink; but righteousness, and peace, and joy in the Holy Ghost." Romans 14:17

The Kingdom in Us

In Luke 19:11, Jesus gave a parable of a master and the servants that were given money to trade with and get more. When the master got back, and followed up. They all presented surplus, except one who hid it. To draw an analogy; the money that these servants were given is the Kingdom of God, the master is Jesus – He came to the earth, brought the Kingdom of God which is the Kingdom of holiness and righteousness, where he is the King and gave it to men. According to Matthew 22:44 Jesus has given us access to the Kingdom of God. We should therefore expand the Kingdom. We should gain more people because the master would be back, that is the second coming of Jesus.

God cannot reign through you if you are an idolater, adulterer, and one who participated in the unlawful living against the word of God. One who does evil cannot get this Kingdom. (1 Corinthians 6:9-10.)

The Kingdom of Heaven is second part of the kingdom that we are conversant which is where the throne of the Lord is. Thy Kingdom come, on earth and it is in Heaven. (Matthew 6:10)

Jesus came from the Kingdom of heaven where holiness, the Glory of the Lord and righteousness dwells, and where God rules (these also makes up the Kingdom of God).

The Apostolic Way

Let's look at the Apostolic Way.

The Apostolic upholds the teachings of the early church. The Apostolic teaches salvation, conviction of sin, repentance and recompense or restoration to our creator. Apostolic people believe in being filled with the Holy Spirit with evidence of speaking and praying in tongues. Most importantly Apostolic embraces the model which the Lord left.

Apostles preach the gospel to every creature, while some denominations/religious do not mix themselves with others and encourage their people to stick to the church home and only that congregation, except for when they are in search of "new members." The Apostles and Apostolic church preach to everyone all the time with no other agenda other than for people to receive Jesus and salvation. Mark 16:15

> "Then he called his twelve disciples together, and gave them power and authority over all devils, and to cure diseases. And he sent them to preach the kingdom of God, and to heal the sick. Luke 9:1-2

> "Afterward he appeared unto the eleven as they sat at meat, and upbraided them with their unbelief and hardness of heart, because they believed not them which had

seen him after he was risen. And he said unto them, Go ye into all the world, and preach the gospel to every creature. He that believeth and is baptized shall be saved; but he that believeth not shall be damned. And these signs shall follow them that believe; in my name shall they cast out devils; they shall speak with new tongues; they shall take up serpents; and if they drink any deadly thing, it shall not hurt them; they shall lay hands on the sick, and they shall recover. So then after the Lord had spoken unto them, he was received up into heaven, and sat on the right hand of God. And they went forth, and preached everywhere, the Lord working with them, and confirming the word with signs following. " Mark 16:14-19

We learn from here that;

- The Apostles are to preach
- People believe
- Signs follow them
- They overcome
- Healing takes place
- Jesus is with them always.

Ephesian 2:5-10 the Bible made us to know that:

- God loves us greatly
- He raised us up and made us sit in heavenly places with Christ Jesus

- He showed us the exceeding riches of his grace in his kindness toward us through Christ Jesus.
- By grace we are saved through faith; and that not of yourselves: it is the gift of God:
- We are his workmanship, created in Christ Jesus unto good works, which God hath before ordained that we should walk in them.

Hallelujah, if we know this we should have no problem fitting into the Kingdom of God.

Chapter Reflections

1. _____

_____

2. _____

_____

3. _____

_____

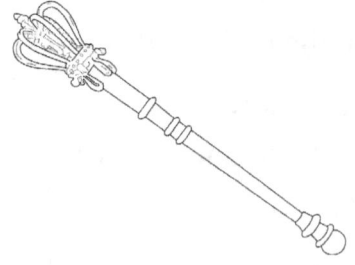

Chapter Three

We Have A Heavenly Father

> "(For after all these things do the Gentiles seek :) for your heavenly Father knoweth that ye have need of all these things."
>
> – Matthew 6:32

Believers have a heavenly Father who knows about all their needs, and cares for them. He is a Father that cannot be compared to any earthly father. His ways are different from the ways of men, and his acts are also different from the acts of men. This is why we should trust him as our Father.

He wants to be our Father, and he is calling us to come to him. 2 Corinthians 6:16 – 18 said, **"And what agreement hath the temple of God with idols? For ye are the temple of the living God; as God hath said, I will** dwell in them, and walk in them and I will be their God, and they shall be my people. Wherefore come out from among them, and be ye separate, saith the Lord, and touch not the unclean thing; and I will receive you, and will be a Father unto you, and ye shall be my sons and daughters saith the Lord Almighty."** He wants us to come out of the dirty and defiled world into holiness and righteousness. This is the only way that he can become our Father.

God Our Father Is Spiritual

The Bible made us to know that our God is a spiritual God. He is not controlled by physical factors, rather, he controls them. Romans 1:20 said, **"For the invisible things of him from the creation of the world are clearly seen, being understood by the things that are made,** *even* **his eternal power and Godhead; so that they are without excuse:"**

He is a God to whom all glory and honor belongs to. He is from everlasting to everlasting, and is infinite in power. He is the **"...King eternal, immortal, invisible the only God"** (I Timothy 1:17**)**

John 4:24 said, **"God is spirit and His worshippers must worship in spirit and in truth."** Our Father in essence is a spiritual being; He is invisible to the eyes of humans but is very real. From a scientific point of view, I have tried to describe briefly this fact of sometime being invisible but still tangible. Our God is able to be touched and experienced by humans.

Consider the infinite amounts of creatures that surround you and live on objects around you for example there are about a million viruses that can live on the surface of the period at the end of this sentence. There are trillions of bacteria on the skin of healthy individuals can you see them? Not without the aid of a highly powered electron microscope. Consider other elements and forces around you, wind; can it be seen other than when it rushes through the leaves of trees or sweeps across your face. It cannot be seen captured in a container but yet it is very real. Or what about electricity, you have never seen it, but yet it exists, and is very tangible. The elements and forces continue on, for example magnetic forces are all real but have never physically been seen.

This particular nature is very vital to an understanding of our Father; how He operates and functions, I am sure you are tried the examples I gave and are probably saying, yeah what is the point? The matter is in Genesis 1:26 and 27 the Bible said, "**And God said, let us make man in our image, and after our likeness: and let them have dominion over the fish, of the sea, and over the fowl of the air and over the cattle and over all the earth, and ever every creeping thing that creepeth upon the earth. So God created man in His own image, in the image of God created he Him: male and female created**

He them." The above Scripture captures brilliantly the essences of our Father who is Lord, sovereign ruler and King. It describes Him as being great and full of power.

Webster's II New Riverside Dictionary describes great as superior, outstanding, eminent or renowned. Our owner and father have a tremendous reputation of being bigger and far superior than the average false being or imaginary gods. He is known for doing grandiose acts; miracles of extreme portions and granting to His children gifts that are far above the thoughts of any human. His future plans for all creation are far beyond what our eyes have seen, ears heard or thoughts that have entered the minds of human. He is that awesome and great!

Our Father Is Full Of Power

The word 'Power' comes from the Lexical Aids to the Old Testament.

Here are the following definitions:

- **Cheryl or Cheryl**: It means strength, valour, military force, army, wealth, virtue and honesty.
- **Chayil** – Might, power, ability.

The main meanings of this noun are "strength", 'army' and 'wealth'.

These Old Testament commutations express a God who has strength, a military fortitude and power from wealth or influence.

New Testaments portrays the power of our Father in Matthew 6:13 and said, **"And lead us not into temptation but deliver us from evil: For thine is the Kingdom, and the power, and the glory, forever. AMEN."** The Bible also said in Revelation 4:11 "Thou art worthy, O Lord, to receive glory and honour and power: for thou hast created all things and thy pleasure they are and were created."

The Lexical Aids to the New Testament describes this power of God as:

- **D!namis**; power. Meaning being able, capable inherent power. This means that He has built into His nature the ability and capacity to do anything. This source of enablement resides and flows from our Father.
- **Exousia from exesti**. The word '**Exousia**' has the meaning of permission, authority, right, liberty, power to do anything. '**Exesti**' expresses the capability or the right to do a certain action.

'**Exousia**' denotes executive power or justified, having the right to exercise power. There the Greek clearly delineates that God has with Himself the power to do anything He wants. He has executive power meaning that it is His inherent right to the world and everything in it. Power was not given or delegated to Him. He has power that is absolute and unrestricted.

The word dominion is another term used for our Father. It comes from the original Greek **Kr"tos**, force, strength, might, more especially manifested power, dominion. '**Kr"tos**' denotes the presence and significance of force or strength.

Some passages of the Scriptures that mentions this includes; I Chronicles 29:11, 12 "**Yours, O Lord is the greatness and the power, and the glory and the majesty and the splendor, for everything in heaven and earth is yours. Yours, O Lord, is the Kingdom; you are exalted as head over all. Wealth and honor come from you; you are the ruler of all things. In your hands are strength and power to exalt and give strength to all.**" We also see in Psalm 45:6 "**Your throne, O God, will last forever and ever; a sceptre of justice will be the scripture of your Kingdom.**" Another place is in Psalm 103:19 "**the Lord has established His throne in heaven and His kingdom rules over all.**" Psalm 145:13 also said, "**Your Kingdom is an everlasting kingdom, and your dominion endures through all generations.**"

Scripture clearly states that our Father is a King. A King is one who has ruler-ship, governs and administrates sovereignty over a territory. Our Father the King from references mentioned above has sovereign rule over the earth, the creatures and over every person. All belong to the owner and master our daddy.

Our father has authority over the earth because He created the earth, the heavens and everything with those regions. He has all rights and privileges to exert His desires and will over the entire creation.

He desires to influence the world and creation with His love, righteousness, justice and holy nature thereby allowing His character to be reflected in all His creation.

A King of Wisdom

In Revelation 7:11-12, the Bible said, "**And all the angels stood round the throne, and about the elders and the four beasts and fell before the throne on their faces, and worshipped God, Saying Amen: Blessings, and glory, and wisdom, and thanksgiving and honour and power and might be unto our God forever and ever AMEN.**"

The writer, John the Beloved, ascribes a glorious worth to our God. He vividly outlines a scene in the heavens that is both futuristic but yet a daily occurrence at the throne room of the Father. John articulates that angles and elders are bowing before the Lord and worshipping Him, they are giving Him the credit and worth due to His name and nature.

They are ascribing to the Father blessings (to innate ability to prosper) glory (weight of wealth and majesty) and wisdom. Our Father rules with wisdom, from His throne over the affairs of creation. He governs with great skill, understanding and wit. This word wisdom means true spiritual and heavenly wisdom. It also denotes skilful expert, sensible, prudent. He is a God that is very skilful in His decisions, Excellent in His operations!!

The Bible said in Proverbs 3:19, 20 (NIV) "**By wisdom the Lord laid the earth's foundations, by understanding he set the heavens in place; By His knowledge the deeps were divided, and the clouds let drop the dew.**" This is the kind of Father that we have.

> "To God belong wisdom and power; counsel and understanding are His." (Job 12:13

We, as His children, can be assured and rest in the confidence that our Father rules our universe, with superior ability and expertise. All decisions that are related to our faith in His direction are made in wisdom. All things in our lives, once we abide by His laws and rules, are being carefully orchestrated by our loving father. One writer says that all things work together for our good to those persons that love the Father; and are called to fulfil the purposes and will of the Father.

Even the most difficult circumstances and situations are being divinely designed to strengthen, empower, increase and propel us into God's divine destiny.

He is mindfully, strategically connecting the dots of our lives to construct a masterful piece of art work. Just trust His word!! The principles in His word, of the Bible are filled with wisdom above the knowledge of this age.

His principles and wisdom where applied consistently and continually daily will lead to a life of fulfilment and purpose. His wisdom gives us as children a tremendous advantage over the outside relatives. These 'outsiders' refers to our brothers and sisters (person who have not accepted the love of their Father through Jesus Christ as Lord and Saviour). These "bastard" children live outside of the wisdom of the Fathers plan and hence experience unnecessary pains and sufferings from the challenges of this life.

But praise God our loving Father, we are being led by a mighty wise King who will cause His children to triumph and excel in the Kingdom He has given to us on this earth. His has given to us authority in the earth to master and challenge our lives with His eternal wisdom.

We learn that Jehovah God is an infinite spiritual being, and that mankind was made in the image and likeness of the Heavenly Father as a spiritual and moral being. God has innate absolute sovereign power to rule the heaven and earth, and executive power to govern everything. He has dominion over the earth and all the creatures (including humanity). Finally, our Father has all wisdom; His knowledge is infinite. Because of who our Heavenly Father is, we should put our trust in him, and he will guide and direct our lives.

Chapter Reflections

1. _____
_____

2. _____
_____

3. _____
_____

Chapter four

The Authority Of The Kingdom Citizens

> "Then he called his twelve disciples together, and gave them power and authority over all devils, and to cure diseases." - Luke 9:1

Every citizen of the Kingdom of God is given authority over every situation. This is unlike what is obtained in the world, as only the government officials or security officers are bestowed with authority. During the ministry of Jesus Christ here on earth, he walked and did his work with authority, and as he was going, he gave that same authority to every believer.

Authority is given to the citizens of the Kingdom of God because they have an arch enemy who is constantly fighting against them.

> "Be sober, be vigilant; because your adversary the devil, as a roaring lion, walketh about, seeking whom he may devour: Whom resist steadfast in the faith, knowing that the same afflictions are accomplished in your brethren that are in the world." 1 Peter 5:8, 9,

It takes God-given authority for one to be able to resist and withstand the devil. People who don't have this authority will always be at the mercy of the devil.

> "Submit yourselves therefore to God. Resist the devil, and he will flee from you." James 4:7

We can only resist the devil when authority is being given to us, because it takes greater power to overcome a strong man in his house.

Another reason why believers are given this authority is for them to make breakthrough while doing the work of the Kingdom. In Acts 13, the Apostle Paul was preaching the Gospel when he was met with opposition through Elymas the sorcerer. If he had not authority, he would have been defeated by Elymas. The Bible gave the account of what happened;

"And when they had gone through the isle unto Paphos, they found a certain sorcerer, a false prophet, a Jew, whose name was Barjesus: Which was with the deputy of the country, Sergius Paulus, a prudent man; who called for Barnabas and Saul, and desired to hear the word of God. But Elymas the sorcerer (for so is his name by interpretation) withstood them, seeking to turn away the deputy from the faith. Then Saul, (who also is called Paul,) filled with the Holy Ghost, set his eyes on him, And said, O full of all subtlety and all mischief, thou child of the devil, thou enemy of all righteousness, wilt thou not cease to pervert the right ways of the Lord? And now, behold, the hand of the Lord is upon thee, and thou shalt be blind, not seeing the sun for a season. And immediately there fell on him a mist and a darkness; and he went about seeking some to lead him by the hand. Then the deputy, when he saw what was done, believed, being astonished at the doctrine of the Lord." Acts 13:6-12

The authority of Paul over the sorcerer made the deputy to believe the Gospel of the Kingdom. As you go preaching the Gospel, you need this authority to be able to silence the gainsayers and detractors.

Authority is also needed to be able to heal the sick, cast out devils, and to work all manner of miracles, signs and wonders. This was why before Jesus Christ sent out his disciples to go and preach the Gospel; he first gave them power and authority to do these things. In Luke 9:1, 2, the Bible said, "**Then he called his twelve disciples together, and gave them power and authority over all devils, and to cure diseases. And he sent them to preach the kingdom of God, and to heal the sick.**"

Think about how embarrassing it will be when one is faced with a sick person while preaching the Gospel, and such person could not heal the sick. It ought not so to be. Authority is needed to be able to experience these signs and wonders.

Authority is the code of life for every citizen of the Kingdom of God. We are given authority to "**trample on serpents and scorpions and over every power of the enemy**". We are called to live in the reality of this authority.

Authority Given By Christ

Jesus Christ manifested authority throughout his ministry. It came to a point that the people acknowledged it and said in Luke 4:36 "...**What words are these! For with authority and power he commandeth the unclean spirits, and they come out.**"

Everything Christ did was done in authority. His teaching was done in authority. Matthew 7:29 said that "...**he taught them as one having authority, and not as the scribes.**" It was this authority that he manifested that made his enemies to be defeated. A time came that the scribes asked him to tell them the nature or source of authority which he manifested. The Bible said in Matthew 21:23, "**And when he was come into the temple, the chief priests and the elders of the people came unto him as he was teaching, and said, By what authority doest thou these things? And who gave thee this authority?**" All these point to the fact that the ministry of Jesus was backed up with divine authority. Knowing the importance of authority, he also gave every citizen of the Kingdom the same authority.

In Matthew 28:18, the Bible said "**And Jesus came and spake unto them, saying, all power is given unto me in heaven and in earth.**" When he said "**all**", he meant that there is nothing beyond or above his power and authority. He meant that he alone has the final say, and because of this, he gave his disciples and in application, to every believer this charge.

> "Behold, I give unto you power to tread on serpents and scorpions, and over all the power of the enemy: and nothing shall by any means hurt you." Luke 10:19

This means that as long as all power and authority belongs to Christ, believers also have all power and authority over the devil and sicknesses.

Manifesting the Authority through Faith

For a believer to see the authority in manifestation, it must be through faith. People who are faithless cannot manifest authority. It takes faith to manifest authority.

> "Above all, taking the shield of faith, wherewith ye shall be able to quench all the fiery darts of the wicked." Ephesians 6:16

Casting out devils for the first time or praying for the sick to be healed demands faith. You to do signs and wonders. When the disciples of Jesus could not cast out the devil in the possessed boy, he called them men of "**little faith**."

As Jesus gave the church the great commission, he told them that only those who believe will be able to experience the signs and wonders. To believe means that when you see the sick, you lay your hands upon them and pray for them. When you see those under satanic or demonic oppression, you command the devils to come out.

> "And these signs shall follow them that believe; in my name shall they cast out devils; they shall speak with new tongues; they shall take up serpents; and if they drink any deadly thing, it shall not hurt them; they shall lay hands on the sick, and they shall recover." Mark 16:17-18

How to Keep Our Authority

Authority can be lost or taken away from an individual. If our authority must be kept, there are some actions or steps that we must take. In Matthew 8:9, the Centurion that came to Jesus said to him, **"For I am a man under authority, having soldiers under me: and I say to this man, Go, and he goeth; and to another, Come, and he cometh; and to my servant, Do this, and he doeth it."** He acknowledged that he was a man under authority, and as long as he remained under authority, he is able to exercise authority over his servants. Jesus Christ himself was a man under the authority of the Father. This was why the Scribes wanted to know the source of his authority.

For believers to keep on manifesting authority, they must remain under the authority of Jesus Christ. Those who go outside the authority of Jesus Christ by disobeying his words cannot exercise authority over sicknesses and evil spirits etc. There must be submission to the Lordship and authority of Christ because all power and authority is given to him.

Another thing that must be done is to continue in holy living.

> "The wicked flee when no man pursueth: but the righteous are bold as a lion." Proverbs 28:1

Holiness and purity of heart gives us authority over the devil.

> "The righteous also shall hold on his way, and he that hath clean hands shall be stronger and stronger." Job 17:9

Sin defiles a believer's authority and renders it ineffective. As long as you continue to live righteously, you will always be able to exercise this God-given authority.

Chapter Reflections

1. _____
_____

2. _____
_____

3. _____
_____

Chapter Five

Papa's Prosperity Plan

> Deuteronomy 8:18 "But thou shalt remember the Lord thy God: for it is He that giveth thee power to get wealth, that He may establish His covenant which He swore unto thy fathers, as it is on this day."

The Scripture declares that we ought to always remember our owner and source. It is through His ability, enablement, access and authority that we get the wealth. He gives His ability, His word, principles and strength for His children to acquire not only physical, emotional, and mental well-being but also financial wealth, praise God!

Father comes to live with His children

"And I will pray the Father, and he shall give you another Comforter, that he may abide with you forever. Even the Spirit of truth; whom the world cannot receive, because it seeth him not, neither knoweth him: but ye know him; for he dwelleth with you and shall be in you." John 14:16-20 (vs. 18) "I will not leave comfortless: I will come to you." (vs. 19) "Yet a little while, and the world seeth me no more, but ye see me: because I live, ye shall live also." (vs. 20) "And that day ye shall know that I am in my Father, and ye in me, and I in you."

John 14:26-27 "But the Comforter, which is the Holy Ghost, whom the Father will send in my name, he shall teach you all things, and bring all things to your remembrance, whatsoever I have said unto you." (vs. 27) "Peace I leave with you, my peace I give unto you: not as the world giveth, give I unto you…"

John 15:26-27 "But when the Comforter is come, whom I will send unto you from the Father, even the Spirit of truth, which proceedeth from the Father, He shall testify of me." (vs. 27) "And ye also shall bear witness, because ye have been with me from the beginning."

John 16:13-16 "Howbeit when He, the Spirit of truth, is come, He will guide you unto all truth: for He shall not speak of Himself; but whatsoever He shall hear, that shall He speak; and He will show you things to come." (vs. 14) "He shall glorify me: for He shall receive of mine, and shall shew it unto you. (vs. 15) "All things that the Father hath are mine: therefore said I, that He shall take of mine, and shall shew it unto you. (vs. 16) "A little while, and ye shall not see me: and again, a little while, and ye shall see me, because I go to the Father.

Daddy is filled with gifts and wonderful surprises for His Sons. He has provided all things for them to enjoy and share. The Father mysteriously now presents the greatest gift of all to His precious children.

I can imagine a wonderful birthday of a young boy as he wakes early and runs excitedly to his parent's bedroom. He is eagerly anticipating the promise of his father. All year long the young lad cleaned his room on time, washed the dishes and did his homework in excellence. Now it was his time to be the recipient of reward by his father. He gently knocks on the bedroom door of his Father and shouts, "Dad, Dad!" his father having anticipated the son's desire for the promised gift cries, "Come on in son!" His son raced through the doors as a horse out of a Kentucky Derby starting gate and galloped towards his father. He leaped into the bed in between his mother and father and melodiously sang, "Did you remember dad?" in the ears of the Father. Lovingly the father stared at his handsome 10-year-old son whose eyes now beamed with joy and whose smile was wider than the Nile River; he replied, "Yes." The father said happy birthday and gently embraced the boy. The Father hurried into a nearby bedroom closet and rolled into the room a 10 speed mountain bicycle sparkling blue with gold trimmings to the lad. His eyes lit up with magnificence as his father said joyously this is your gift son, I remembered my promised. Without hesitation the son jumped on the bicycle; his father stood by with a smile as was overwhelm with the excitement of the son. Immediately the writer Luke's analogy popped into my mind; and clearly outlined the nature of the Father.

> "If you then, being evil, know how to give good gifts unto your children: how much more shall your heavenly Father give the Holy Spirit to them that ask Him? Luke 11:13

Jesus strongly states that men and earthly fathers are moved with fulfilment when they give their children gifts. They get joy from things that would make them happy, increase their value and gifts that would propel their children dreams. Jesus reveals the agape level of love in this verse; in that the heavenly Father gives the most powerful person and tool for the ultimate fulfilment of purpose of His children.

The Heavenly Father gives Himself in the person of the Holy Spirit to dwell with His Sons forever. Let us clarify how He does this mysterious and marvellous event.

The writer John in **I John 5:7**, *"For there are three that bear record in heaven, the <u>Father</u>, the <u>Word</u> and the <u>Holy Ghost</u>: and these three are one."*

> (vs. 11) "And this is the record that God hath given to us eternal life, and this life is in His son." (vs. 12) "He that hath the Son hath life: and he that hath not the Son of God hath not life."

John expresses that the Father, the Word (Jesus) and the Holy Spirit are one. They have the same vision but different functions but yet still remain the same. It is a mystery!!! There is then eternal life in the Son as the Son gives us the Holy Spirit as we will examine. The Father knows how to give the gift of Himself to be an advisor forever with His Sons in the Earth. John the writer records the most profound words of Jesus as He expresses the wondrous plans and purposes of the Father towards mankind.

In **John 14:15-20 (vs. 15)** *"If ye love me, keep my commandments,*

> (vs. 16) "And I will pray the Father and He shall give you another Comforter that he may abide with you forever;(vs. 17) "Even the Spirit of truth; whom the world cannot receive, because it seeth Him not, neither knoweth Him, but ye know Him; for He dwelleth with you, and shall be in you."(vs. 18) "I will not leave you comfortless: I will come to you." (vs. 19) "Yet a little while, and the world seeth me no more; but ye see me: because I live ye shall live also."(vs. 20) "At that day ye shall know that I am in my Father, and ye in me, and I in you." (vs. 21) "He that hath my commandments, and keepeth them, he it is that loveth me: and he that loveth me shall be loved of my Father and I will love him, and will manifest myself to him."

Here is the passion and intent of the Father that by abiding and living by the commandments the Father will give His Sons the Holy Spirit. Here we see Jesus petitioning the Father to send the perfect gift of the Holy Spirit to be with the believer forever. Praise God! Jesus truly gives His best to His Sons. The Holy Spirit—man's greatest gift!!

Amazingly, Jesus elaborated on the relationship of the Holy Spirit with His children; the Holy Spirit will not just rest upon the believer temporally or visit the children of

God in a Sunday service. Neither will He just show up to give the believer a jump or a shout. The Holy Spirit was given to the Sons of God to dwell in the children hearts. He will be their closest confidant, friend and advisor.

What an awesome privilege!! Sadly, the world, the bastard children, those not in conventional relation or identity with the Father cannot see Him, the Holy Spirit or perceive Him. The Father was so concerned and mindful of His intimate relationship, He did not want to leave us anymore. He wanted to be next to and inside His children forever. Praise God He has far surpassed any earthly father or false God. There is no other claim of other gods as Jesus' claims of what the Father has done by living in His children forever.

John 14:19 expresses the uninterrupted relationship the Father wants. He states that He would never leave His children comfortless; meaning there will never be a moment that He wants His Sons to be out of peace with themselves or external circumstances. Jesus begins to speak about the gift of the Holy Spirit and the intermixing He wants for Sons with the Father and the Holy Spirit. **Verse 20** states, *"At that day ye shall know that I am in my Father, and ye in me and I in you."*

Praise God, the Father with Jesus and the gift (Holy Spirit) desire oneness that would cause a power unity a marriage that would complete the love relationship of the Father.

In fact, Jesus promises that the sons that keep the commandments and love Him will have reciprocal love streaming down from His throne that will saturate their lives. Jesus will also flood His sons with an abundance of 'agape' love relationship love and concern. He will also reveal His nature, purpose and secrets to the obedient Sons.

> John 14:26 "But the Comforter, which is the Holy Ghost, whom the Father will send in my name, He shall teach you all things, and bring all things to your remembrance, whatsoever I have said unto you."

> John 15:26 "But the comforter is come, whom I will send unto you from the Father, even the Spirit of truth, which proceeded from the Father, He shall testify of me."

John expounds that the gift, the Holy Spirit has functions while He lives and abides in the life of the believer.

Jesus describes the Holy Spirit in **John 16:14-15**, *"He shall glorify me: for He shall receive of mine, and shall show it unto you."*

> (vs. 15) "All things that the Father hath are mine: therefore said I, that he shall take of mine, and shall shew it unto you.

The key to developing any firm relationship is communication. This involves both verbal and non-verbal uses of symbols, language and speech to portray ones concept and meaning. This form of communication the Father wanted expressed by Jesus is a constant dialogue with His Holy Spirit. He knew that He was returning to the Heavenly Father after completing His purpose and mission in the earth and was about to engage in a new work as the Chief Intercessor for the Sons of God.

Our heavenly Father's intention for the creation was relationship and not a dictatorship for man. The Father sent the gift of the Holy Spirit to assist in cultivating and maintaining a line of communication and intimacy with His children. Amidst intimacy come strong family ties, identity as with a clearer understanding of the other persons involved. With the contents of a natural family, moments share in activity or simply talking forges bonds between members. These bonds are emotional and individuals have the opportunity to express feelings of anger, disappointment, satisfaction and joy in a loving environment. The Lord our Father is quite the same; desiring to be an active father, friend, confidant in our lives.

He desires to reward obedience, correct our errors and foster our dreams and destinies. There is a tremendous blessing for obedience to the voice of the Spirit of our Father.

> "O righteous Father, the world had not known thee: but I have known thee, and these have known that thou have sent me." John 17:25

The Father's intention for His prize children He created was for intimated relationship, fellowship, and not dictatorship. Let us look at the Father's yearning to be our sources, progenitor and daily nourisher through the Holy Spirit.

> "And what agreement hath the temple of God with idols? For ye are the temple of the living God; as God hath said, I will dwell in them, and walk with them; and I shall be their God, and they shall be my people." (vs. 17) "Wherefore come out from among them, and be ye separate, saith the Lord, touch not the unclean thing; and I will receive you, (vs. 18) And will be a Father unto you, and ye shall be my sons and daughters saith the Lord Almighty." II Corinthians 6:16-18

Paul the writer of Corinthians challenges the church at Corinth to avoid being unequally yoked together with unbelievers in **verse fourteen**. He unlocks the mysterious of Christ and the indwelling of the Holy Spirit sent from the Father in the believer. Paul metaphorically relates our bodies as the temple or the place where the divine meets the natural man, of the Father.

"... Ye are the temple of the living God..."

The Holy Spirit who is living, a being that lives, feels, is offended, and desires to live in the Sons. He the Holy Spirit says *"I will dwell in them and walk in them..."* Amazing He will be their God. The Almighty King of the Universe states, that *"He shall be the faithful father unto His Sons and daughters."* He has taken full responsibility of being the source of all His children. Praise God saints, you don't have to look into the oblivion of the skies and seek daddy. Just realize that His Holy Spirit is right next to you to hear all of your concerns. He wants to celebrate with your victories and successes in life; grieve with you hurt and comfort you in distress.

Praise God look inside you; He dwells not in the temple of stones as in the old covenant, but through the request of Jesus, He lives forever in us His Sons!

Praise God look this moment and acknowledge the presence of the Holy Spirit right next to you as you read these words and worship the King and Father who abides in your inner being. Go on just love on Him for a minute.

The children of God are as carriers of royalty, majesty, glory and transporters of the King. We change the atmosphere when you step into a room or circumstance because you carry God in you. Every circumstance of life must bow in the presence of the King. Greater is He that is in you than any person or situation facing you. You are a God carrier of His glorious presence! Sons are an ark of the presence of God.

Chapter Principles

- Our heavenly father is infinitely wealthy and wants to share His riches with His children in the earth.

- The father's greatest gift is to His entrance in the earth as Jesus.

- The Father's awesome gift was to live inside the life of every believer of Jesus Christ.

- The Father dwells in His sons as the Holy Spirit.

- The Holy Spirit is the director advisor and comforter who is the exact nature as Jesus.

- The Holy Spirit of Jesus only speaks and directs in the purpose if the Father.

- Humans can now connect with the destiny of the Father for them through submission to the Holy Spirit.

Chapter Reflections

1. _____
_____

2. _____
_____

3. _____
_____

Segment Two

Resurrection Power

Chapter Six

Power Of Resurrection

> "But if the Spirit of him that raised up Jesus from the dead dwell in you, he that raised up Christ from the dead shall also quicken your mortal bodies by his Spirit that dwelleth in you." – Romans 8:11

*J*esus Christ is the only one who describe with certainty what will happen after death. He told His disciples and the people He was going to die and resurrect back to life. Other pioneers of different religions of the world could not talk about what happens after death with certainty. They only had speculations about their past. With audacity, Jesus spoke about the things that will happen after His death, and it happened exactly the way He said it.

He had so much power in Him such that when He died, even those who were dead came back to life When He rose on the third day, others rose with Him. Their decayed body was restored.

Imagine seeing people who were dead walking around the city. This was the first evidence of the resurrection power of Jesus Christ. Jesus has the power of resurrection. His death unlocked this power, and created the possibility for every saint to have eternal life.

Why Jesus Had To Come

Without the shedding of blood, there is no remission of sin. The wages of sin is death. This means without sin you cannot die. Jesus had no sin. The Bible says:

> "The Lord God planted a garden eastward in Eden, and there He put the man whom He had formed. And out of the ground the Lord God made every tree grow that is pleasant to the sight and good for food. The tree of life was also in the midst of the garden, and the tree of the knowledge of good and evil. Then the Lord God took the man and put him in the Garden of Eden to tend and keep it. And the Lord God commanded the man, saying, "Of every tree of the garden you may freely eat; but of the tree of the knowledge of good and evil you shall not eat, for in the day that you eat of it you shall surely die." (Genesis 2:8-9; 15-16 NKJV)

Imagine that man was made in the image and likeness of God. Adam was made in the image of God. The question is whose blood flows through the body of a child? Medically, the blood of the mother and that of the baby should not mix. Therefore, a baby has the blood of the father. For Adam, he had the blood of God.

Jesus is the second Adam. He did not have a biological father. Mary was a surrogate mother. Medical science taught us that the child and mother's blood should not mix. It can be fatal and deadly. Jesus had the blood of the eternal Father.

For Adam and Eve. God told them not to eat the fruit that they would die. But the Serpent seduced and beguile Eve. We need to understand that the Serpent cannot attack anyone until he speaks the person out of God's Word. The serpent lied to her that they would not surely die. The Bible says;

> "Now the serpent was more cunning than any beast of the field which the Lord God had made. And he said to the woman, "Has God indeed said, 'you shall not eat of every tree of the garden'?" And the woman said to the serpent, "We may eat the fruit of the trees of the garden; but of the fruit of the tree which is in the midst of the garden, God has said, 'You shall not eat it, nor shall you touch it, lest you die.'" Then the serpent said to the woman, "You will not surely die." (Genesis 3:1-4 NKJV)

We should also correct the popular misconceptions about the fruit they ate. Adam and Eve did not eat any apple. They ate the fruit of the tree of knowledge of good and evil. This corrupted their sense of glory, and they fell from the glory and purity of God.

The Devil asked them, "Did God say?" Satan cannot tempt you outside God's Word. The Word of God came directly and clearly to Adam and Eve, but they disobeyed. He corrupted their perception of death, and deceived them.

The wages of sin is death. Sin did not contaminate Jesus' blood, because He lived a sinless life and was of the Father. According to spiritual laws, sin gives way to death. Adam and Eve sinned, and all humanity sinned as a result (Ecclesiastes 7:20, Romans 3:10). We were conceived, shaped and born in iniquity. We had the nature of sin because of Adam. Jesus did not have the sin nature in Him, and was without blemish. There is power and purity His blood to cleanse, purify, redeem and reconcile humanity back to God.

Jesus did not have the nature of Adam. This was why He said no man could take my life, I lay it down. Death could not touch Him. Nails did not kill Him. He laid His life down. The resurrection power of Jesus also tells us more about the power at work in him. Over 700 people saw Jesus after resurrection. If Jesus had remained in the grave we would not have been saved.

Jesus Can Raise the Dead

According to Medical Science, after four days, a dead body begins to decompose. No wonder what happened when Jesus came to raise Lazarus from the death. When Mary and Martha asked Jesus why He did not come early when Lazarus was sick, He said it was for the Glory of God. Jesus said He is the resurrection and the life. Jesus made this statement when He was yet to die. He is not the resurrection because He died but because He lives.

Martha knew about the resurrection. She told Jesus that she knew about resurrection that Lazarus will be raised together with the saints during the resurrection but Jesus displayed another phase of resurrection this fateful day. Resurrection is not just an event; it is a person. Jesus proved that he was the awaited resurrection, and he raised Lazarus from death. Praise the Lord!

Jesus is the first begotten of the dead, the first fruit of the dead. Jesus said I am the first who died, raised from the dead and live– he lives forevermore. Many people were raised to life through Jesus. Elijah also raised the dead to life. Abraham had an understanding of resurrection before Jesus came to life. He knew God was able to raise Isaac if he killed him. God stopped him, and commended his faith.

Jesus believed in the power of His revelation. However, He knew that revealing it to the disciples was not enough to keep the testimony of his resurrection, so he appeared to many more people. That is Power!

He Is Eternally Alive

I have thought about the early Christians, why they would be ready to face persecution and death. Why they did not deny their faith? Well, I have come to realize that they had powerful testimonies from their encounter with Jesus. Why they were willing to be tortured, thrown to the lion's, burnt, beaten? Why the Roman Empire and the Pharisees and Sadducees were willing to kill them? This is because they had so much convictions that nothing could be taken away from them. They were able to endure all these because they were not only able to see Jesus; they saw the resurrected Christ. I pray that you will also encounter the resurrected Christ (Amen).

An encounter with the resurrected Christ is enough to keep us on fire for the cause of the Gospel. We are to be witnesses. Not just about preaching, but professing the reality of His resurrection.

Here are some scriptural evidences of his resurrection:

> "And as they went to tell His disciples, behold, Jesus met them, saying, "Rejoice!" So they came and held Him by the feet and worshiped Him. Then Jesus said to them, "Do not be afraid. Go and tell my brethren to go to Galilee, and there they will see Me." (Matthew 28:9-10 NKJV)

"After that, He appeared in another form to two of them as they walked and went into the country. And they went and told it to the rest, but they did not believe them either." (Mark 16: 12-13 NKJV)

"And how the chief priests and our rulers delivered Him to be condemned to death, and crucified Him. But we were hoping that it was He who was going to redeem Israel. Indeed, besides all this, today is the third day since these things happened. Yes, and certain women of our company, who arrived at the tomb early, astonished us." (Luke 24:20-22 NKJV)

"And they said to one another, "Did not our heart burn within us while He talked with us on the road, and while He opened the Scriptures to us?" 33 So they rose up that very hour and returned to Jerusalem, and found the eleven and those who were with them gathered together, saying, "The Lord is risen indeed, and has appeared to Simon!" And they told about the things that had happened on the road, and how He was known to them in the breaking of bread."(Luke 24:32-35 NKJV)

Then He said to them, "These are the words which I spoke to you while I was still with you, that all things must be fulfilled which were written in the Law of Moses and the

Prophets and the Psalms concerning Me." And He opened their understanding, that they might comprehend the Scriptures. Then He said to them, "Thus it is written, and thus it was necessary for the Christ to suffer and to rise from the dead the third day, and that repentance and remission of sins should be preached in His name to all nations, beginning at Jerusalem. And you are witnesses of these things. Behold, I send the Promise of My Father upon you; but tarry in the city of Jerusalem until you are endued with power from on high." (Luke 24:44-49 NKJV)

Others verses: Acts 2:31; Acts 4:2; Acts 4:33.

Jesus Christ in indeed risen, and he lives forevermore. Those who believe in Him will also have eternal life. That same power can also heal our mortal bodies when we are sick. All we need to do is to believe. May you believe and your eyes be open to the reality of this awesome power.

Chapter Reflections

1. _____

_____

2. _____

_____

3. _____

_____

Chapter Seven

The Resurrection And Demonstration Of Jesus' Kingdom Power

Ever since the fall of man, the expression of God's redemptive agenda seemed to be existing like a suspense. From the foundations of the earth, the blood of the Lamb of God had been shed, even though it was yet to become visible to mankind. Man, being God's special creation was so loved by God, that God kept sending men to help others out of their various challenges. There were great leaders that arose amongst the people, there were priests, judges, kings, prophets and prophetesses, great teachers of the law, warriors and mighty men of valour, hence, none of these ones could give man the permanent redemption.

However, in order to redeem the life of men, the life of a man had to be shed. Not just an ordinary man, but a man that had the life of God. God had to come to the earth by himself through Jesus Christ. He lived among men for over three decades. In the last three years of His existence on earth, His ministry on earth was revealed. He went about doing good, with the anointing of the Holy Ghost that was upon Him. After doing many mighty wonders on earth, it was time to proceed to doing the major assignment that brought Him. He was subjected to the threat of men. He was arrested, beaten, crucified, and then gave up His life. It was right there on the cross that the redemptive work started;

> "Blotting out the handwriting of ordinances that was against us, which was contrary to us, and took it out of the way, nailing it to his cross; And having spoiled principalities and powers, he made a shew of them openly, triumphing over them in it. (Colossians 2:14-15)

Before His death, He had already declared that He would rise back to life, and those in authority in their own cunning way had positioned soldiers at His tomb, so that no one would take Him away and claim that He had risen. Having spent three days in the grave, Jesus Christ, the Son of the Living God came back to life. The very big stone that was placed at His tomb was rolled away. The soldiers that were positioned at His tomb were just like dead men. They reported to their employers that He truly resurrected. They were paid to lie that He was taken away by His disciples when they were asleep, hence, to prove His resurrection to those who doubted it. He began to appear to them, not in dreams or visions; but physically.

In Mark 16, on the day after Sabbath, Mary Magdalene and other women went to the tomb of Jesus with spices to anoint His body, only for them to discover that the stone had been rolled away. Entering the tomb, they saw an angel who told them that Jesus Christ whom they sought had risen from the dead.

Eventually, He began to appear to His disciples. First amongst them was Mary, from whom He had cast out seven demons. Although, when she told others about the fact that Jesus was alive because He had appeared unto her, they found it so difficult to believe. In order to help their unbelief, Jesus appeared again to two of His disciples in the 12th and 13th verses, and in spite of their account, the others still refused to believe. And then, the 16th verse of Mark 16 reveals that Jesus Christ would not leave them to their state of unbelief, as He appeared to the eleven as they sat at the table. And then, having rebuked their unbelief, He gave unto them, the great commission.

In Luke's account of the resurrection, the 24th chapter from verse 36, Jesus appeared in the midst of His disciples. Of course they were afraid and terrified, hence, they could still not believe that it was not His spirit that appeared unto them. Jesus however showed His feet and hands to them, to see the signs of the nails. Having said that, He discovered that they needed more proof and so He demanded for food. They gave Him food and He ate right there before them, just for Him to be able to prove to them that it was Him in their midst and not the spirit of the dead.

John, one of the writers of the synoptic Gospel also gave an account of how Jesus appeared to Simon Peter and other disciples at the Sea of Tiberas. After they had done all they could to get fish as professional fishermen, they caught nothing. Jesus appeared to them, and He asked them to cast their net on the right side. And when they did, they caught a lot of fishes. It was at that instance that they recognized Him, and even thereafter, He ate breakfast with them.

Paul the Apostle, in his first epistle to the Corinthian church, in the 15th chapter, from the first verse to the eleventh verse, gave a synopsis of how Jesus Christ's resurrection was confirmed by various apostles, including himself. He emphatically said in the sixth verse, that at a time, He even appeared unto five hundred brethren at once.

One mystery that is needed to be well understood is that, Jesus Christ was not killed by men, He rather gave up His life for men. That which happened at the cross and in the grave had been written. He only came to fulfil that which had been said, and concluded before the foundations of the earth.

> *He rather gave up His life for men.*

Jesus did not become the resurrection after He rose up from death, He was already known as the Resurrection and the Life even before His death. This He confirmed when He was about to raise Lazarus from being dead. He said; "I am the resurrection and the life". His supremacy over death did not start after visiting the Hades, He already has the power over death before death was created. He only won that victory for humanity.

In Hebrews 2:14-18, the present ministry of Jesus was revealed. In the days of the ancient priests, the priests themselves needed to purify themselves before appearing before the Lord for the people. God would pass His instructions and reveal His intentions through the sanctified priest. Any priest who entered into the Most Holy Place without being sanctified properly would not be able to come out alive. At that time, they depended solely on the blood of animals for their consecration. Jesus Christ, would not need to die again and again, neither would any other sacrifice be needed for the atonement of sins.

Right now in the Presence of God, Christ is seated as an advocate, interceding on behalf of the Saints before the Father. There is no priest that is as effective as He is. There is no one that can solicit for us like He presently does.

> *He already has the power over death before death was created.*

He is our High Priest, who had been tempted just as we are, He knows what we go through, for he had been through the same while on earth. He is our High Priest without any sin or blemish. Just as the Holy Ghost is advocating for us on earth, He is presently advocating for us in Heaven.

Colossians 2:13-15 revealed those things that the death and resurrection of Jesus Christ did to the Kingdom of Darkness and for the Saints who believe in the Kingdom of God. We can therefore say that the following had been achieved through the death and resurrection of Jesus Christ;

- He spoiled principalities and power
- He made an open show of Satan
- He destroyed the fear of death
- He took the keys of hell and death(Rev. 1:17-18)
- He gave us access to the throne of God(Hebrews 4:14-16)
- As our High Priest, He is currently making intercessions on our behalf

The following scriptures also confirm that Jesus is our High Priest;

- Hebrews 7:21-28
- Hebrews 9:11-28

There used to be a testament, which was in existence before Jesus came. That testament depended on the blood of animal for the consecration of the people. But then, Jesus' blood became the foundation of the New Testament, and it is on this foundation that the Gospel is established. Right now, every one of us has been purchased from death and hell by the blood of Jesus. We used to be under the influence of sin and the fear of death, hence, by the blood of Jesus Christ, we had been saved, we had been transformed; we had been purchased and no price can be higher than the blood of Jesus that will be able to buy us back into the Kingdom of Darkness.

> *No price can be higher than the blood of Jesus.*

If we have this kind of liberty and we keep it to ourselves, then, we can be described as selfish. Jesus, before descending to Heaven, charged His disciples to "Go into the world and preach the Gospel to all nations..."(Matthew 28:19-20). The salvation that Jesus gave through His life is not only meant for a group of people, but for the whole human race. How then can people know that they had been saved, unless someone preach the message of the Gospel to them? Having known the resurrection power of Jesus Christ, it is quite important that we spread the light of the Gospel to others who are yet to believe.

It is also very important for us to know that the Kingdom of God is not far away in Heaven, as the Kingdom

> God is not only in Heaven, but right here inside us.

of God is in us (Luke 11:20). Jesus, before He left said that He had to go, so that the Holy Ghost might fully come. This became a reality on the day of Pentecost, when the Apostles were gathered in the same place, and the Holy Ghost came upon them. It was because Jesus Christ had completed His assignment on earth that the Holy Spirit was able to fully come upon men. It is important to emphasis whenever we witness unto men that God is not only in Heaven, but right here inside us. We don't have to get to a special place of worship before we worship and commune with God; for the Spirit of God in us makes intercessions on our behalf.

Having talked about Jesus' existence, His death and resurrection, and even the manifestation of the Holy Ghost in these present dispensation, our witnessing is incomplete if we do not add the fact that Christ Jesus is coming back again. 1 Corinthian 15:52 reveals to us how quick it shall happen. In a twinkling of an eye, at the sound of the last trumpet, the dead shall rise back to life..." We cannot complete our witnessing to men without duly informing them that life does not end where they think it ends. The world needs to know that indeed, there is life after death. There is a need for us to emphasis that only those who believe in Jesus Christ would be partakers of the eternal life of God that is to come after now. We cannot shy away from the reality of hell, we cannot but tell men that those who eventually get condemned would spend eternity in hell where there is an eternal furnace that cannot be quenched.

> *The world needs to know that indeed, there is life after death.*

Through the power of Jesus Christ, every believer is equipped to be able to heal the sick and to raise the dead. Through the advantage that we had received through the blood of Jesus Christ, we are unharmed even when we get poisoned. Through His power we have authority over all the power of the enemy. Evil should never be able to consume the believer's life.

Chapter Reflections

1. _____

_____

2. _____

_____

3. _____

_____

Chapter Eight

The Blood Of Jesus: Why The Blood Of Jesus Is So Powerful

Jesus is the most under-studied and misunderstood character of authority. A lot of people spend much time studying celebrities, sport leaders, professional leaders, government officers, athletes and Christian leaders such as the pastors, bishops and even the church organizations. It is crucial to take an in-depth study on the personality of Jesus Christ, His ministry and calling so that we may truly know Him.

> [For my determined purpose is] that I may know Him [that I may progressively become more deeply and intimately acquainted with Him, perceiving and recognizing and understanding the wonders of His Person more strongly and more clearly], and that I may in that same way come to know the

power outflowing from His resurrection [which it exerts over believers], and that I may so share His sufferings as to be continually transformed [in spirit into His likeness even] to His death, [in the hope] (Philippians 3:10 AMP)

The Name of Jesus

In the New Testament, Jesus is translated as 'Iesous' meaning Jehovah is Salvation or Jehovah Saves. In the Old Testament, Jesus can be translated to the English word 'Joshua'. In Hebrew, it means 'Yehoshua' meaning Jehovah is Salvation. Christ is 'Christos' the anointed one. 'Messiah' is translated as 'the King of Israel.' The 'Mashiach' translated as the consecrated person or one who is King; set apart or consecrated.

We must return to our first love; making Christ the center. We are experiencing a lot of brokenness in the world because man decided to take the place of Christ. Extolling Christ in every affair of life will restore all the brokenness in the world. We must bring to an end the worship of man 'human worship' in the church which is equivalent to the sin of idolatry. We must return to Jesus the author and finisher of our faith. This does not mean that we should disrespect our neighbors and church authorities but to focus our gaze on Jesus. Focusing our gaze on Jesus keeps us from discouragement. This is not a guarantee that we would not face trials but an assurance that we will overcome every trial that comes our way.

The Blood of Jesus

In the beginning, God created man to be sinless just as He is but man lost this position in the Garden of Eden because he fell, as a result of disobedience.

> For Adam also and for his wife the Lord God made long coats (tunics) of skins and clothed them (Genesis 3:21 AMP).

As a result of the fall, their eyes were opened and they were ashamed. God had to make a coat of skin to cover the nakedness of man. This implies that God instituted the use of the blood for the remission of sin which is later confirmed in the book of Hebrews 'without the shedding of blood, there is no remission of sins.'

> [In fact] under the Law almost everything is purified by means of blood, and without the shedding of blood there is neither release from sin and its guilt nor the remission of the due and merited punishment for sins (Hebrews 9:22 AMP).

This is not man-made but a divine principle. Jesus Himself was slain even before the foundations of the world;

His blood was shed for us to make an eternal covenant with the Father. In Genesis 4:10 it was established that blood is living and can speak.

> And [the Lord] said, what have you done? The voice of your brother's blood is crying to Me from the ground (Genesis 4:10 AMP).

> And Noah built an altar to the Lord and took of every clean [four-footed] animal and of every clean fowl or bird and offered burnt offerings on the altar (Genesis 8:20 AMP).

> Then Moses called for all the elders of Israel, and said to them, Go forth, select and take a lamb according to your families and kill the Passover [lamb]. And you shall take a bunch of hyssop, dip it in the blood in the basin, and touch the lintel above the door and the two side posts with the blood; and none of you shall go out of his house until morning. For the Lord will pass through to slay the Egyptians; and when He sees the blood upon the lintel and the two side posts, the Lord will pass over the door and will not allow the destroyer to come into your houses to slay you (Exodus 12:21-23 AMP).

The priests were also responsible for the administration of blood sacrifices to the Lord.

Now the main point of what we have to say is this: We have such a High Priest, One Who is seated at the right hand of the majestic [God] in heaven, As officiating Priest, a Minister in the holy places and in the true tabernacle which is erected not by man but by the Lord. For every high priest is appointed to offer up gifts and sacrifices; so it is essential for this [High Priest] to have some offering to make also. If then He were still living on earth, He would not be a priest at all, for there are [already priests] who offer the gifts in accordance with the Law. [But these offer] service [merely] as a pattern and as a foreshadowing of [what has its true existence and reality in] the heavenly sanctuary. For when Moses was about to erect the tabernacle, he was warned by God, saying, See to it that you make it all [exactly] according to the copy (the model) which was shown to you on the mountain. But as it now is, He [Christ] has acquired a [priestly] ministry which is as much superior and more excellent [than the old] as the covenant (the agreement) of which He is the Mediator (the Arbiter, Agent) is superior and more excellent, [because] it is enacted and rests upon more important (sublimer, higher, and nobler) promises. For if that first covenant had been without defect, there would have been no room for another one or an attempt to institute another one. However, He finds fault with them [showing its inadequacy] when He says, Behold, the days will come, says the Lord, when I will make and ratify a new covenant or agreement with the house of Israel and with the house of

Judah. It will not be like the covenant that I made with their forefathers on the day when I grasped them by the hand to help and relieve them and to lead them out from the land of Egypt, for they did not abide in My agreement with them, and so I withdrew My favor and disregarded them, says the Lord. For this is the covenant that I will make with the house of Israel after those days, says the Lord: I will imprint My laws upon their minds, even upon their innermost thoughts and understanding, and engrave them upon their hearts; and I will be their God, and they shall be My people. And it will nevermore be necessary for each one to teach his neighbor and his fellow citizen or each one his brother, saying, Know (perceive, have knowledge of, and get acquainted by experience with) the Lord, for all will know Me, from the smallest to the greatest of them. For I will be merciful and gracious toward their sins and I will remember their deeds of unrighteousness no more (Hebrews 8:1-12 AMP).

Jesus is our High Priest making intercessions for us. He desires to be our God with His words written on the tables of our hearts. Through the death and resurrection of Jesus, a new covenant was established.

The blood of Jesus is stronger than the blood of animals; through his blood He secured an eternal redemption for us. If the blood of animals was able to heal, deliver and cleanse sins in the Old Testament, how much more the blood of Jesus Christ! Through the blood of

Jesus that purges we have the ability to turn from sins and serve the living God.

Medically, the blood of the mother does not mix with the fetus. The blood of the fetus is formed when the fetus is developed. At the moment of conception, the baby has its own blood that is developed. The mother provides nutrients to the fetus but the blood forms in the embryo by itself. When Jesus was born, he did not have the blood of His earthly father Joseph nor of His earthly mother Mary. He had a divine blood! He walked through his earthly ministry with uncontaminated blood which made Him the perfect sacrifice for all. Moses sprinkled blood in the tabernacle with the blood of animals for sanctification but we are sanctified through the offering of the blood of Jesus once and for all (Hebrews 10:35) because His blood is without sin.

We need to develop the habit of applying the blood of Jesus. It is sufficient for our healing and protection. Through the sacrifice made by the blood of Jesus, we have boldness to access the throne of grace.

> Therefore, brethren, since we have full freedom and confidence to enter into the [Holy of] Holies [by the power and virtue] in the blood of Jesus, By this fresh (new) and living way which He initiated and dedicated and opened for us through the separating curtain (veil of the Holy of Holies),

that is, through His flesh, And since we have [such] a great and wonderful and noble Priest [Who rules] over the house of God, Let us all come forward and draw near with true (honest and sincere) hearts in unqualified assurance and absolute conviction engendered by faith (by that leaning of the entire human personality on God in absolute trust and confidence in His power, wisdom, and goodness), having our hearts sprinkled and purified from a guilty (evil) conscience and our bodies cleansed with pure water (Hebrews 10:19-22 AMP).

So let us seize and hold fast and retain without wavering the hope we cherish and confess and our acknowledgement of it, for He Who promised is reliable (sure) and faithful to His word.

According to Hebrews 10:20 our hearts have been sprinkled from an evil conscience by the blood of Jesus but sin will give us a conscience of guilt which winder us from accessing the throne of grace with confidence. The devil is specialized in reminding us of our sins because he knows the power we will receive at the throne of grace.

By this fresh (new) and living way which He initiated and dedicated and opened for us through the separating curtain (veil of the Holy of Holies), that is, through His flesh (Hebrews 10:20 AMP).

We must learn to activate our position in Christ. Tap into the power of forgiveness that lies in the blood of Jesus. We must learn to pray with confidence and boldness (Hebrews 10:23). In Hebrews 4:14-16, we are made to understand that we have a faithful High Priest who is touched by our infirmities, pains and temptations. Let us make it a habit to relay our challenges to the Lord. He understands how we feel and He is ever ready to hear and answer us when we call (Hebrews 5:1, Mark 14:24, Luke 22:20). We are also blessed with spiritual blessings and adopted in Christ Jesus.

The blood of Jesus gives eternal life through communion (Acts 20:28, Romans 3:25, 1Corithians 10:16, 1Corithians 11:25).

> And Jesus said to them, I assure you, most solemnly I tell you, you cannot have any life in you unless you eat the flesh of the Son of Man and drink His blood [unless you appropriate His life and the saving merit of His blood]. He who feeds on My flesh and drinks My blood has (possesses now) eternal life, and I will raise him up [from the dead] on the last day. For My flesh is true and genuine food, and My blood is true and genuine drink. He who feeds on My flesh

and drinks My blood dwells continually in Me, and I [in like manner dwell continually] in him. Just as the living Father sent Me and I live by (through, because of) the Father, even so whoever continues to feed on Me [whoever takes Me for his food and is nourished by Me] shall [in his turn] live through and because of Me. This is the Bread that came down from heaven. It is not like the manna which our forefathers ate, and yet died; he who takes this Bread for his food shall live forever. He said these things in a synagogue while He was teaching at Capernaum. When His disciples heard this, many of them said, this is a hard and difficult and strange saying (an offensive and unbearable message). Who can stand to hear it? [Who can be expected to listen to such teaching?] (John 6:53-60 AMP).

The blood of Jesus is mysterious. It gives power to overcome every enemy of life (the accuser of the brethren).

And they have overcome (conquered) him by means of the blood of the Lamb and by the utterance of their testimony, for they did not love and cling to life even when faced with death [holding their lives cheap till they had to die for their witnessing] (Revelations 12:11 AMP).

Then war broke out in heaven; Michael and his angels went forth to battle with the dragon, and the dragon and his angels fought. But they were defeated, and there was no room found for them in heaven any longer. And the huge dragon was cast down and out—that age-old serpent, who is called the Devil and Satan, he who is the seducer (deceiver) of all humanity the world over; he was forced out and down to the earth, and his angels were flung out along with him. Then I heard a strong (loud) voice in heaven, saying, Now it has come—the salvation and the power and the kingdom (the dominion, the reign) of our God, and the power (the sovereignty, the authority) of His Christ (the Messiah); for the accuser of our brethren, he who keeps bringing before our God charges against them day and night, has been cast out! (Revelations 12:7-10 AMP).

The blood of Jesus is our defense as believers. It is in the blood of Jesus we have access to the fulfillment of our divine promises in Christ. Making the use of the blood of Jesus consistently gives us victory in all ramifications.

THE SUPERNATURAL POWER OF THE BLOOD OF JESUS

> "Having therefore, brethren, boldness to enter into the holiest by the blood of Jesus"- Hebrews 10:19

How do we know if a being is alive? The proof of life in any being is the flow of blood in that being. In the beginning, God formed man from the dust, the skeletal frame of man had been made, but there was man, lifeless, until God's breath entered into him through his nostrils; and that was when blood began to flow in man.

> "For the life of the flesh is in the blood, and I have given it to you upon the altar to make atonement for your souls; for it is the blood that makes atonement for the soul.'... For it is the life of all flesh. Its blood sustains its life. Therefore I said to the children of Israel, 'You shall not eat the blood of any flesh, for the life of all flesh is its blood. Whoever eats it shall be cut off.'" (Leviticus 17:11; 14 NKJV)

Talking about the power of the blood, God said to Moses in the passage above that the life of a being is in its blood. Therefore, when Jesus gave His life to us, He shed His blood for us, and it is by virtue of that blood that was shed that we have access to God, and victory over the devil.

> "And there was war in heaven: Michael and his angels fought against the dragon; and the dragon fought and his angels, and prevailed not; neither was their place found any more in heaven. And the great dragon was cast out, that old serpent, called the Devil, and Satan, which deceiveth the whole world: he was cast out into the earth, and his angels were cast out with him. And I heard a loud voice saying in heaven, now is come salvation, and strength, and the

kingdom of our God, and the power of his Christ: for the accuser of our brethren is cast down, which accused them before our God day and night. And they overcame him by the blood of the Lamb, and by the word of their testimony; and they loved not their lives unto the death." (Revelation 12:7-11 NKJV).

In the Bible passages above, there is the record of the war that broke out in Heaven. The saints of God appeared to have overcome in the battle, and the 11th verse reveals how they gained their victory; "And they overcame him (the dragon) by the blood of the Lamb and by the word of their testimony..." It is therefore important to note, that one of the greatest advantages derived from the blood of Jesus is the overcoming power.

By virtue of the power in the blood of Jesus, we can rest assured of victory over the enemy. No matter what anyone might be going through, be it anxiety or depression, there is power in the blood of Jesus to overcome. They have told certain people in the past that they have issues in their bloodline. No matter what had been said about your bloodline, the blood of Jesus is able to purify and cleanse you; His blood is able to make you whole.

The Uniqueness of the Blood

There is something quite significant about the blood of Jesus. Therefore, we can say, that the blood of Jesus is capable of cleansing even the blood of any other person. If there were any curse, any kind of guilt, any dominance of fear, whatsoever it might be, the blood of Jesus is able to overcome them all.

> *There is power in the blood of Jesus to overcome.*

The blood of Jesus is without any blemish, unlike the blood of any other being. This is because Jesus was not born by virtue of any sexual activity, unlike every other being. How can this be possible? It was not only possible with Jesus; it was also possible with Adam. Adam, the first man that ever lived, had blood flowing in his body, but he was without any parent. Both he and Eve his wife were living beings, yet, they had no parents. Their life came from God; their blood was pure and holy. No wonder, Jesus was referred to as the second Adam, because his existence was just like that of the first Adam. Hence, it was because the first Adam had fallen, that was why the second Adam, Jesus Christ, came (1 Cor. 15:45).

The Reason for the Blood

We can find the record of the fall of man in the book of Genesis chapter three. After the serpent deceived Eve to eat the "forbidden" fruit, she also gave her husband. After they had eaten the fruit, their eyes opened, and they found out that they were naked. As a way of covering their shame, they went to hide themselves from the presence of God. The beings that had the "blood of God" flowing in them could no longer stand before His presence. Their blood became corrupt because of disobedience, sin began to rule in the affairs of humanity, and there had been many redemptive approaches, which were like palliative measures, as none had been effective like the blood of Jesus.

> The Bible said, "Then Noah built an altar to the LORD, and took of every clean animal and of every clean bird, and offered burnt offerings on the altar. And the LORD smelled a soothing aroma. Then the LORD said in His heart, "I will never again curse the ground for man's sake, although the imagination of man's heart is evil from his youth; nor will I again destroy every living thing as I have done." (Genesis 8:20-21 NKJV).

After God had destroyed mankind using the flood, Noah, being the only righteous man in his days, alongside his family, were the only survivors. After the flood, Noah offered sacrifice to God, and God made a covenant with him and his descendants, which was sealed by the blood of an animal. One thing to understand about covenants is that, there can never be a covenant without blood. A covenant is an agreement between two entities, with the two having a part to play in the agreement plan. In most spiritual contexts, if not all, blood is needed to seal up the covenant. Meanwhile, since it is ungodly for any man to take the life of another man, the blood of certain animals may be required to seal up the covenant.

The Old Covenant with Israel

Genesis 15 records the covenant of God with Abram. As a seal for the covenant, Abraham– as he was later called, used the blood of a three-year-old heifer, a three-year-old female goat, a three-year-old ram, a turtledove, and a young pigeon. God asked Abram to cut them in pieces, and sacrifice them on an altar. Eventually, Abram fell asleep, he woke up to see vultures around the altar, and he chased them away. God made a pronouncement concerning the descendants of Abram; he said that they were going to be slaves in a strange land for four hundred years.

However, in Genesis 17, God approached Abram again, and made another covenant with him. At that time, the sign of covenant was the circumcision of all male children, which must be kept forever as an everlasting covenant. Circumcision requires the cutting away of the upper layer of the male's penis; hence, this cannot be done, without the blood flowing out of that region.

In Exodus 12, a great historical event in the land of Israel began. They had been strangers in the land of Egypt, a strange land just as God had said that they would.

It was time for them to leave, and after nine plagues, Pharaoh, the king of Egypt, was not willing to let them go. God was set to visit the land of Egypt with just one more plague; the death of all firstborn throughout the land of Egypt. In order to ensure that no Israelite family experiences the plague, God recommended that they kill a lamb and mark their doorpost with its blood. God said, **"When I see the blood, I will pass over..."** (Exodus 12:13). That blood was a sign that sealed the covenant of protection against the plague.

Moreover, while in the wilderness, as recorded in Exodus 24:8, God made a covenant with His people as He instructed Moses to sprinkle the blood on them. Then, in verse 8, Moses said, **"...Behold, the blood of the covenant which the Lord has made with you according to all these words"**.

In the days of the Kings of Israel, they offered sacrifices, as atonement unto God. Just as the law, which was given to Moses, they offered sacrifices to God anytime they had sinned and they needed to appeal to Him for the forgiveness of their sins. They also offer sacrifices anytime they had been defiled by an infection, or contact with any unclean person or thing. However, this system of redemption was stressful and costly, they kept offering sacrifices and spilling the blood of animals as required by the law, but then, that was not giving them a permanent redemption.

The prophets began to prophesy the coming of the Messiah. In their days, they were talking about what was to come, and their prediction was said to be the perfect redemption plan. In their various prophecies, most especially, the prophet Isaiah, emphasis was laid on the activities of the coming King, His birth, earthly ministry, death, and resurrection.

The New Blood Covenant through Christ

Glory to God! The prophecies came to fulfillment! Christ Jesus came, walked on the surface of the earth as a Rabbi. Eventually, He gave His life after accomplishing His earthly ministry. His blood was shed once and for all. He is the Lamb of God that was slain, for the remission of our sins. We were bought out of the rule of darkness, and the price for our dying soul was the precious blood of Jesus Christ.

It is important for us to understand that:

- The Blood of Jesus is pure and holy
- The Blood of Jesus is sinless
- The Blood of Jesus is precious
- The Blood of Jesus is the ransom for our dying soul
- The Blood of Jesus is powerful to save and deliver
- The Blood of Jesus does not lose its power; it's ever working
- The Blood of the Lamb(Jesus) had been shed even before the earth ever existed

- The Blood of Jesus brings salvation
- The Blood of Jesus brings healing
- The Blood of Jesus gives redemption
- The Blood of Jesus is the seal of the New Covenant
- The Blood of Jesus empowers us to overcome the devil

> "Therefore, holy brethren, partakers of the heavenly calling, consider the Apostle and High Priest of our confession, Christ Jesus" (Hebrews 3:1 NKJV).

The Bible introduces us to another High Priest that is greater than Moses is. The truth is that no High Priest is as great as Christ is; Christ is the only High Priest that is sinless. No pastor is higher than Christ is! No church leader is greater than Christ is! As a matter of fact, every great leader that the church has ever produced were born in sin, lived in sin, got redeemed from sin by the blood of the Lamb, and looking up to Christ; the only High Priest that has no record of sin.

> "For we do not have a High Priest who cannot sympathize with our weaknesses, but was in all points tempted as we are, yet without sin." (Hebrews 4:15 NKJV)

This verse gave us a clearer picture of the kind of High Priest that we can find in Christ. The fact that Jesus Christ is sinless does not mean He does not understand what it means to be tempted. Just as we are currently being tempted, He was equally tempted as we are. He passed through the same things that we are currently facing. He was God in man's flesh when He was here on earth, He faced all that we are facing, and by the help of the Holy Spirit, He was able to prevail. We have confidence in His blood; knowing that when He died, the veil to the holiest place in the Temple was torn. This signifies access to God's presence. By the new covenant made with His Blood, we can rest assured of access to the presence of God.

> *He is the Lamb of God that was slain, for the remission of our sins.*

Right now, just as we have the Holy Spirit right here inside us on earth, we also have Christ over there in Heaven, beside the Father, interceding for us. Anytime we go astray and we call upon His Name, the Father remembers of the Holy Blood of the Son that has saved and redeemed us from sin. That is why we must;

> "Come boldly to the throne of grace, that we may obtain mercy and find grace to help in time of need" (Hebrews 4:16).

Any life that is sold to sin is sick. In fact, the man with the greatest sickness is the one who is yet to surrender his life to the lordship of Christ. Painfully, many people are still struggling with sin; many are still trying to live righteously. One very powerful understanding that is very important to have is the understanding of what Christ has already done for us.

> He "bore our sins in his own body on the tree, that we having died to sins, might live for righteousness - by whose stripes you were healed" (1 Peter 2:24).

In John 6:48-58, Jesus introduced Himself strangely by saying, **"I am the bread of life"**. Well, what do we do with a bread? He said; "anyone who eats my flesh and drink my blood abides in me and I in him". What a strange description! Jesus is saying, that His blood can also be seen from the perspective of a drink, which if taken, one would be guaranteed of having eternal life. If the life of a being is in its blood, then Jesus is saying, **"drink my blood"**, that means, Jesus is saying; *"have my life in you; believe in what my blood is able to do for you; then, you will have eternal life"*. What a blood!

Prophesying about Jesus, Prophet Isaiah gave us an insight to what is blood is able to do in Isaiah 53:5; **"But He was wounded for our transgressions, He was**

bruised for our iniquities; the chastisement for our peace was upon Him, and by His stripes we are healed". What a very powerful blood!

Many scriptures reveal the power in the blood of Jesus. The following are the summaries of what these scriptures reveal.

- 1 John 7: The Blood cleanses
- Ephesians 1:7: Redemption through the Blood
- Ephesians 2:12-13: The Blood draws us closer to God
- Hebrews 10:19: The Blood grants us access to God
- Colossians 1:20: Through the Blood, we reconcile with God.

With these and many more revealed about the Blood of Jesus, it is important to note that the fact that a believer is not living by the understanding of what the Blood is able to do does not mean that the Blood is powerless. When we come into the understanding of what the Blood of Jesus has secured for us, we are able to approach life differently. The Blood of Jesus is supernatural, and powerful!

POWER OF THE BLOOD OF JESUS

God found a suitable price that could be paid for us —the blood of His only begotten Son, and God so loved us that he gave His only begotten Son (John 3:16). The Bible says, "You have been bought with a price" (1Corinthians 6:20, 7:23) and "God purchased his called out people with his own blood" (Acts 20:28).The heavenly song praises Jesus, "You purchased for God with your blood men from every nation" (Revelation 5:9). When Jesus faced his own death, he spoke of his "blood... shed for many for the remission of sins" (Matthew 26:28).

The Bible says, "Behold the kindness and the severity of God" (Romans 11:22). God's severity demands that a price be paid for us. But God's kindness pays for us the price that we could not find anywhere else. And this price is called "redemption" for the payment of our purchase price. Jesus is our "justification, sanctification, and redemption" (1Corinthians 1:30). This redemption, or buying of freedom, is ours because the blood of Jesus Christ was shed on the cross. Jesus Christ paid the price for us which we could not give in exchange for our own souls.

As Christians, we believe that Christ's body was killed, and his blood shed, as a perfect sacrifice for us. We believe in no other means by which our sins, which alienate us from God, can be forgiven and our guilt removed. We have faith in the blood of Jesus (Romans 3:23-25a).Our sins were "washed away" and they are gone; they are no more through the shedding of Jesus' blood on the cross. As Christians we should not forget this great sacrifice and how God loves us so much and He gave us His only son.

As Christians, we know about the blood of Jesus Christ, we sing hymns about the blood, and remember it during

Communion (although some Christians do forget about this). But most of us do not know how deep its power runs, and all that the blood has provided for us. So many of us don't even know how to use and apply it in our lives every day?

> *Every time we apply the blood, we experience an outpouring of this great love.*

From the Bible (Genesis to Revelation), the word the blood are kept before our eyes—a reminder of its importance and significance to us and to God. The sacrifices of some great men of old like; Abel, Noah and Isaac, and the Passover lamb, and the giving of the Law all came to pass, but "not without blood" (Hebrews 9:7, NKJV). The blood stands for cleansing and purification—the settling of a matter.

The nature of God is love, God is love. And this love was expressed by Him sacrificing His son on the cross to shed His blood for us. This very love covers every need man has had or ever will have. Every time we apply the blood, we experience an outpouring of this great love. This great act is an act of love, through the blood, that has created a barrier between you and all the works of the devil.

Let's put the blood of Jesus Christ to the same place in our hearts that it has in God's very heart—and awaken in our spirits those great and mighty things the blood has procured for us. The power of the blood of Jesus has given you everything you need to live a life of victory, including redemption, fellowship, healing, protection and authority over the devil.

What is the blood of God?

The blood of God which is referred to as the blood that Jesus shed on the cross is the basis of the New Covenant. The night before He was to be crucified, Jesus gave to His disciples a cup of wine and said to them, "This cup is the new covenant in my blood, which is poured out for you" (Luke 22:20). And the pouring of the wine in the cup stands for the blood of Christ which would be poured out for all who would ever believe in Him.

When Jesus shed His blood on the cross, He did away with the Old Covenant requirement which is the continual sacrifices of animals. Their blood was no longer sufficient to cover the sins of the people, because sin against a holy and infinite God requires a holy and infinite sacrifice. "But those sacrifices are an annual reminder of sins, because it is impossible for the blood of bulls and goats to take away sins" (Hebrews 10:3).

While the blood of bulls and goats were a "reminder" of sin, "the precious blood of Jesus Christ, a lamb with no blemish or defect" (1Peter 1:19) The Lord Jesus Christ, paid in full the debt of sin we owe to God, and we no longer need to further make sacrifices for sin. Jesus said, "It is finished" as He was dying, and He meant just that—the entire work of redemption was completed forever by this great sacrifice, "having obtained eternal redemption" for us (Hebrews 9:12).

> *New covenant in my blood, which is poured out for you.*

Why is blood important to human?

Blood is a very important fluid for the body. Life is in the blood. The human blood has four major components: plasma, red blood cells, white blood cells, and platelets. The blood has a lot of functions, which includes: transporting oxygen and nutrients to the lungs and tissues. It helps in forming blood clots to prevent excess blood loss. It also helps to carry cells and antibodies that fight infection. Even the blood of Jesus does much more for you. Your blood actually says who you are. Very little amount of your blood can be taken for a test and someone can clinically detect what is wrong with you in your body.

The importance of the blood of Jesus

The Blood Has Life

The Bible makes us to understand that;

- ...for the life of the flesh is in the blood (Leviticus 17:11);
- ....for it is the life of all flesh (Leviticus 17:14);
- ...for the blood is the life (Deuteronomy 12:23).
- There is life in the blood that was shed for you.

The Blood Speaks

A tragic event happened within the first family living on the Earth among the offspring of Adam and Eve. The fall of man and the introduction of sin into the world brought about every known problem to families throughout human history. In Genesis 4, the Bible told us a story of Cain killing his brother Abel. The Lord came to Cain and said to him "The voice of thy brother's blood crieth unto me from the ground." There is a principle in the Old Testament scriptures that life is in the blood (Leviticus 17:11). Not only is there life in the blood, but innocent blood when spilled to the earth is said to speak. Apparently, blood that is shed on the Earth speaks and it is heard in Heaven. And we can say that, maybe Abel's blood was speaking and crying, "guilty; avenge me; punish him" in God's ears. Whatever it cried it got God's attention and blood must be able to testify or witness something to God. This is why the act of abortion is so detrimental. If you find that you played any role in the abortion of a child, you can confess and repent before the Lord and ask him for forgiveness. Also, ask him to break the curses and consequences that came in to your life as a result of whatever role you played.

The book of Hebrews tells the story of a particular Blood that was shed but this time it was shed for the payment for our sins Hebrews 9:15-23. The blood that Jesus shed was not only poured out on earth but it was also poured into heaven itself. Jesus Christ is a mediator of a blood covenant Hebrews 12:14. The blood of Jesus testifies, speaks and cries better things than that of the blood of Abel which may have said, "Give me justice, avenge me, and punish them." But the blood Jesus cries, "Mercy, mercy, mercy." "Give them mercy." The Blood of Jesus witnesses and testifies in the ears of God, in the court of heaven, and in the face of the accuser, which is Satan.

Innocent blood when spilled to the earth is said to speak.

We do not have to plead our case anymore, because the blood of Jesus Christ pleads our case. We add our testimony to the blood that speaks better things than what the blood of Abel spoke (Revelation 12:11). We confess our sins and we are cleansed by the blood John 1:9. God gives us mercy and not what we do deserve because of the blood. The Blood Jesus cries mercy on our behalf. And we thank God for the Blood that Jesus shed.

The Blood Became a Price for our sin

1 Corinthians 6:20 "You were bought with a price. Therefore glorify God in your body and in your spirit, which are God's". Apostle Paul reminded us that we were bought with a price. Yes, it cost God something to redeem us, God paid the price by sacrificing His son for us. "We were bought" in that verse means that our redemption did

not come without a price being paid by God, it was not free for God.

This price that was paid to redeem us, set us free from the wrath and penalty of sin and reconcile us back to God was the cost of "Blood" that was shed by God's own Son, Jesus Christ at Calvary while we were yet sinners when we were separated from God because of our sins.

Hebrews 9:12-14 "Neither by the blood of goats and calves, but by his own blood he entered in once into the holy place, having obtained eternal redemption for us. For if the blood of bulls and of goats, and the ashes of a heifer sprinkling the unclean, sanctifieth to the purifying of the flesh: How much more shall the blood of Christ, who through the eternal Spirit offered Himself without spot to God, purge your conscience from dead works to serve the living God?"

The Blood Symbolizes an Agreement or Covenant

The first covenant appeared with Noah (Gen. 8:20). Noah offered sacrifice to God after the flood, and the term "covenant" came to become God's commitment to never again destroy the world by flood. The new covenant agreement was secured through the death of Jesus on the cross at Calvary. This covenant was greater than the first covenant, it superseded it, as Jesus Christ paid the price of people's sin by laying his life and offering it as a perfect sacrifice. This was different from the old covenant as

Jesus did not take the blood of bulls and goats and ashes of burnt heifer to offer as a sacrifice, but his blood to secure forgiveness for whoever believe in Him.

The Blood of Jesus Gives Power Over the Devil

It is the blood of Jesus that Satan fears. Revelation 12:11 says, "And they overcame him [Satan] by the blood of the Lamb ..." The devil doesn't really want you to learn about the blood. He hates it when you know it! Satan knows that there is victory in the blood of Jesus, and when you make good use of it, you have victory by the blood of Jesus, so he wouldn't want you to know about the power and victory in the blood of Jesus.

There's Victory in the Blood

"They overcame him by the blood of the Lamb, and by the word of their testimony; and they loved not their lives unto death" (Rev. 12:11). In "the blood of the Lamb," each Christian always has victory through the blood of the holy Lamb that was slain on the rugged cross at Calvary. It is when;

- the soul of man is convinced of this power which the blood has with God, in heaven, to effect a perfect reconciliation, and
- the blotting out of sin; and
- to rob the devil of his authority over us completely and forever; and

- to work out in our hearts a full assurance of the favor of God; and
- to destroy the power that sin has – it is,
- When the soul lives in the power of the blood, in that the temptations and tricks of Satan cease to ensnare.

Where the holy blood of the Lamb is sprinkled, there God always dwells, and Satan is put to flight and then you have victory. In heaven, and on earth, and in our hearts, that word as the announcement of a progressive victory that is valid: "They overcame him by the blood of the Lamb."

Victory is through faith, that is, when we truly believe. "This is the victory that overcometh the world, even our faith. Who is he that overcometh the world, but he that believeth that Jesus is the Son of God?" (1 John 5:4-5). "Be of good cheer," said our Lord Jesus, "I have overcome the world" (John 16:33). Satan is an already conquered enemy, a looser from the beginning. He has nothing, absolutely nothing by right, to say to one who belongs to our Lord Jesus. You may give the devil authority over you through unbelief, or by ignorance of, or letting go of the fact that you have a participation in the victory of Jesus. But when you know, by a living faith, that you are one with the Lord Jesus, and that the Lord Himself lives in you, and that He maintains and carries in you that victory which He gained, then Satan has no power over you. Hallelujah! Victory "by the blood of the Lamb" is the power of your life, it's the power you have over the already defeated devil, you only need to believe and make good use of the victory already obtained over the devil through the blood of Jesus.

Only this faith can inspire courage and joy in you to thrive. By thinking of the terrible power of the enemy, of his never-sleeping watchfulness, of the way in which he has already taken possession of everything on earth by which to tempt us, it might well be said – as some Christians think – that the strife is too severe, it is not possible to live all the time under such tension, that life would be impossible. This is perfectly true, if we in our weakness and imperfections had to meet the enemy, or gain the victory by our own might. But that is not what we are called upon to do. Jesus is the Victor; so we need only to have our souls filled with the heavenly vision of Satan being cast out of heaven. Being filled with faith in the blood by which Jesus Himself conquered, and with faith that He Himself is with us, to maintain the power and victory of His precious blood. Then we also "are more than conquerors through Him that loved us" (Rom. 8:37).

POWER OF THE BLOOD TO DELIVER

The power in the name of Jesus is powerful, we are victorious through the finished works of Jesus on the cross. Jesus is more than able to save us from any and every

Don't be like the people of this world

human affliction. He grants us freedom, freedom from economic slavery, freedom from self-identity slavery and every form of slavery you can think of.

God saved the children of Israel by delivering them physically out of Egypt. He saves us today by delivering us spiritually out of this present evil world. (Galatians 1:4). When we accept Jesus as our Lord and personal Savior, God gives us the Holy Spirit in return and then translates us into the Kingdom of God. (Colossians 1:13); a Spiritual Kingdom which is not of this world. (John18:36).

The world hated Jesus and also crucified him. This evil act crucifies believers to the world. (Galatians 6:14). It ensures we neither love the world, nor the things of the world. Thus, John warns: "If anyone loves the world, the love of the Father is not in him." (1 John 2:15).Jesus overcame the world. He says: "If the world hates you, you know that it has hated me before it hated you."(John 15:18). Paul also counsels: "Don't be like the people of this world, but let God change the way you think."(Romans 12:2).

The Gospel makes us to understand that man is already dead. We are "dead in our trespasses and sins." (Ephesians 2:1). Jesus came to this world, He saves from this living death state and by raising the dead back to life. He declares: "I am the Resurrection and the Life! He who believes in me, though he die, yet he shall live. And whoever lives and believes in me shall never die." (John 11:25-26). He even allowed himself to be killed on the cross at Calvary. However, he rose triumphantly from the dead. So doing, he exposed the lie of counterfeit death. Through Jesus, we made to discover that what we fear as death is actually no more than sleep. The real and true death comes from separation from God. Jesus "died to rescue all of us who live each day in fear of dying."(Hebrews 2:15).

> "The blood will be a sign for you on the houses where you are, and when I see the blood, I will pass over you. No destructive plague will touch you when I strike Egypt. "This is a day you are to commemorate; for the generations to come you shall celebrate it as a festival to the LORD—a lasting ordinance. For seven days you are to eat bread made without yeast. On the first day remove the yeast from your houses, for whoever eats anything with yeast in it from the first day through the seventh must be cut off from Israel. On the first day hold a sacred assembly, and another one on the seventh day. Do no work at all on these days, except to prepare food for everyone to eat; that is all you may do. "Celebrate the Festival of Unleavened Bread, because it was on this very day that I brought your divisions out of Egypt. Celebrate this day as a lasting ordinance for the generations to come. In the first month you are to eat bread made

without yeast, from the evening of the fourteenth day until the evening of the twenty-first day. For seven days no yeast is to be found in your houses. And anyone, whether foreigner or native-born, who eats anything with yeast in it must be cut off from the community of Israel. Eat nothing made with yeast. Wherever you live, you must eat unleavened bread." Then Moses summoned all the elders of Israel and said to them, "Go at once and select the animals for your families and slaughter the Passover lamb. Take a bunch of hyssop, dip it into the blood in the basin and put some of the blood on the top and on both sides of the doorframe. None of you shall go out of the door of your house until morning. When the LORD goes through the land to strike down the Egyptians, he will see the blood on the top and sides of the doorframe and will pass over that doorway, and he will not permit the destroyer to enter your houses and strike you down." Exodus 12:13-23 NIV

The blood is the life given element to every animal. Some people actually faint at the sight of it, but no one can live without it! The blood consist of red and white blood cells floating in a liquid called plasma. The red blood cells serves as a kind of delivery system. They carry oxygen and other nutrients to all the cells in one's body, and also helps to carry away all the waste, like carbon dioxide. Blood is pumped through your body by the help of the heart. Your heart is a strong muscle, and it's also fast.

— It can pump blood to every cell in your body in less than a minute! Blood travels through tubes called blood vessels, and the vessels that carry blood away from your heart are called arteries, while the ones that carry it back to your heart are called veins. The white blood cells are the warrior cells. They work together with your immune system to fight off germs and diseases. They fight diseases in your system even before you know of it.

Your blood is powerful and also very important. But the blood of Jesus is even more powerful, capable of redeeming, cleansing, healing and delivering. Because Jesus is the Son of God, He lived a perfect life, and never sinned — not even one single time — His blood is capable of carrying your sins away and gives you the forgiveness you need to live forever with the great God. All you need to do is believe and obey Him. When He gave His life for you on the cross, it was both terrible and beautiful—terrible for the way Jesus was hurt, but so beautiful for the gift of love and forgiveness and heaven He gave to you and me.

Platelets are another very important part of your blood. When you get a cut or scrape, the platelets spring into action, sticking together to stop the flow of blood — called clotting. They do not only keep blood inside your body but also keep germs out of your body. We cannot live without our blood and we can't live eternally in Heaven with God without the blood of Jesus. The blood of Jesus is the best gift we have ever received! It's so amazing!

The process of God's redemption of Israel gives us an example of how He redeems every sinner by Jesus Christ. Israel's redemption is beautifully divided into two different aspects, helping us to clearly see all that is included in the great work of salvation God has provided for mankind.

Two Aspects of Redemption

The first aspect of God's redemption of Israel concerns blood. Exodus 12 records that each household was to kill a lamb and apply the blood that lamb to the upper and side posts of their doors. Without the shedding and application of the blood every Israelite family would have also lost the firstborn of their children and of their animals. There was no deliverance for the children of Israel without the shedding and application of the blood of a lamb.

This shedding of blood typifies the shedding of Christ's blood for the forgiveness of our sins. Hebrews 9:22 says, "And almost all things are by the law purged with blood; and without shedding of blood is no remission [forgiveness]." The blood of Jesus that was shed provides deliverance from condemnation for all who trust Him as Lord and Savior. John 5:24 records the words of Christ regarding this matter: "He that heareth my word, and believeth on him that sent me, hath everlasting life, and shall not come into condemnation; but is passed from death unto life." Deliverance from condemnation is possible only because Jesus shed His blood for us on the cross at Calvary—"while we were yet sinners, Christ died for us" (Rom. 5:8).

The second phase of salvation concerns power. By the power of God, He delivered the Israelites from the slavery of Egypt and then He took them to the desert for training. Where they depended totally on God's leadership and power for all of their needs. In the same way, the individual believer of today needs to rely totally on God for power in daily living. Salvation in Christ makes one a "new creature" (II Cor. 5:17), and the believer needs to realize that "all things are of God" (v.18). The leadership and the power of God are provided for the believer in the death and resurrection of Jesus Christ and it is effected by the Holy Spirit who has been given to us.

Chapter Reflections

1. _____
   _____

2. _____
   _____

3. _____
   _____

Chapter Nine

Experiencing The Power Of God

The question is not "How do we get supernatural power from God?" The question is, "What type of person do we need to be for God to trust us with His power?"

If we are going to learn how to walk in the experience of God, then we will need to learn to walk hand in hand with God. The power of God is given by Him. It is not something we earn or manipulate with a formula. It is something we learn to walk in as we learn to walk with Him.

It takes determination and meditation in the Word of God to cultivate the areas of our lives that will bring the blessing of God. But as we become more and more determined we will experience more and more of God's mighty power at work in each aspect of our lives.

1. ***Find the promises given by Jesus about receiving power from God.*** They are in Luke 24:49 and Acts 1:8

   "And, behold, I send the promise of my Father upon you: but tarry ye in the city of Jerusalem, until ye be endued with power from on high", Luke 24:49

   "But ye shall receive power, after that the Holy Ghost is come upon you: and ye shall be witnesses unto me both in Jerusalem, and in all Judea, and in Samaria, and unto the uttermost part of the earth." Acts 1:8

2. Notice that the verse in Luke associates' power with "the promise (Jesus) Father" and the one in Acts associates the power with receiving the Holy Spirit.

3. Notice that in Acts 1:4-5 Jesus identified the promise of the Father as the baptism of the Holy Spirit, so that we can now see that the "power" comes from the same source: the baptism (or receiving) of the Holy Spirit.

In Acts 2:4 the disciples received power when they received the Holy Spirit; they also spoke in tongues. In Acts 2:38 Peter tells us how to receive power by telling us how to receive the Holy Spirit.

4. ***Seek more information on how to receive this power, the Holy Spirit, go to How to Receive the Holy Spirit as per The Bible.*** Then when you have received the power from God you can start using it to glorify God and win people to Him.

5. ***Understand that when you receive the Holy Spirit you've entered into something so big it's beyond comprehension.*** And I pray that you and all God's holy people will have the power to understand the greatness of Christ's love—how wide, how long, how high, and how deep that love is. Christ's love is greater than anyone can ever know, but I pray that you will be able to know that love. Then you can be filled with everything God has for you. With God's power working in us, he can do much, much more than anything we can ask or think. (Ephesians 3:18-20)

6. ***Use the power to heal the sick.*** Verily, verily, I say unto you, He that believeth on me, the works that I do shall he do also; and greater works than these shall he do; because I go unto my Father. John 14:12

> Now unto him that is able to do exceedingly abundantly above all that we ask or think, according to the power that worketh in you. Ephesians 3:20

7. ***Use the power to preach God's word.*** But ye shall receive power, after that the Holy Ghost is come upon you: and ye shall be witnesses unto me both in Jerusalem, and in all Judaea, and in Samaria, and unto the uttermost part of the earth. Acts 1:8

> And my speech and my preaching was not with enticing words of man's wisdom, but in demonstration of the Spirit and of power. Corinthians 2:4

8. ***Use the power to give witness to Jesus and attract people to God.*** Now when he was in Jerusalem at the Passover, in the feast day, many believed in his name, when they saw the miracles which he did. John 2:23

And the people with one accord gave heed unto those things which Philip spoke, hearing and seeing the miracles which he did. Acts 8:6

> For our gospel came not unto you in word only, but also in power, and in the Holy Ghost, and in much assurance; as ye know what manner of men we were among you for your sake. Thessalonians 1:5

9. *Use the power to give witness of salvation.*

> For I am not ashamed of the gospel of Christ: for it is the power of God unto salvation to everyone that believeth; to the Jew first, and also to the Greek. Romans 1:16

> For the preaching of the cross is to them that perish foolishness; but unto us which are saved it is the power of God. Corinthians 1:18

Jesus taught that the kingdom of God worked from within.

He said, Matthew 13:33:

> "The kingdom of heaven is like leaven, which a woman took and hid in three measures of meal till it was all leavened"

It doesn't take long before a little leaven will affect the whole piece of dough.

The laws and principles of God's Kingdom continue to work in every part of our lives as long as we continue in His Word. *The first important tool that will help us experience God's power is learning to meditate on God's Words.* Meditation will activate ideas within us that will be inspired by God.

The second tool that will help us experience God's power is speaking in tongues which God has given us. God makes available to every believer a supernatural language to enable him/her to pray God's perfect will from his spirit.

> 1Corinthians 14:2 says, "for he who speaks in a tongue does not speak to men but to God, for no one understands him; however, in the spirit he speaks mysteries"

As we meditate upon and yield ourselves to God's Word, we will find ourselves praying in the Spirit for God's perfect will for both ourselves and others. It is a precious gift from God that will build us up. Jude 20 says, "But you, beloved, build yourselves up [founded] on your most holy faith [make progress, rise like an edifice higher and higher], praying in the Holy Spirit"

A third aspect that will help us experience God's power is to diligently attend to matters involving our money. If we will follow God's directions concerning finances, we will find the wisdom of God and the blessings of God will come upon us.

It is also important to remain in a giving attitude. God will direct us to give continually. But He will also show us how to receive. He will adjust our thinking to correspond to His thoughts. Isaiah 55:8 says, "For My thoughts are not your thoughts, nor are your ways My ways." As we meditate in God's Word our thoughts will be adjusted and we will begin thinking His thoughts.

It is also important to remain in a giving attitude.

Proverbs 13:4 says, "The soul of a lazy man desires, and has nothing; but the soul of the diligent shall be made rich." In this passage, God is revealing to us one of the secrets to increasing in His abundance. We cooperate with Him through our complete willingness to follow His direction.

Then we begin to think as He does.

"The plans of the diligent lead surely to plenty, but those of everyone who is hasty, surely to poverty" (Proverbs 21:5 NKJV).

Our thoughts are seeds. The closer our thoughts become like God's, the more seed we are planting into our lives. Then those seeds of plenty produce a great harvest. That harvest is the reward of diligence.

Chapter Reflections

1. _____

2. _____

3. _____

Chapter Ten

Miracles Of The Kingdom

> "How great are his signs! And how mighty are his wonders! His Kingdom is an everlasting Kingdom, and his dominion is from generation to generation." - Daniel 4:3

The *Kingdom of God* is known is for miracles, signs and wonders. When Jesus was here in earth, his ministry was characterized with various miracles, and signs happening. Daniel 4:3 said, **"How great are his signs! And how mighty are his wonders! His kingdom is an everlasting kingdom, and his dominion is from generation to generation."** In the Kingdom of God, nothing is impossible, because with God, all things are possible. Miracles happening was a common occurrence in the ministry of Jesus that the Bible said in Acts 10:30 that, **"How God anointed Jesus of Nazareth with the Holy**

Ghost and with power: who went about doing good, and healing all that were oppressed of the devil; for God was with him."** That same power is still working miracles in this Kingdom.

Miracles Take Place in the Kingdom

As Jesus preached the Kingdom of God, he backed it up with power by manifesting signs and wonders. When Peter later gave account of his ministry, he said in Acts 2:22, **"Ye men of Israel, hear these words; Jesus of Nazareth, a man approved of God among you by miracles and wonders and signs, which God did by him in the midst of you, as ye yourselves also know:"** The miracles that Jesus did were open miracles that the rulers of the Jews couldn't hide it anymore. The Bible said in John 11:47, **"Then gathered the chief priests and the Pharisees a council, and said, what do we? For this man doeth many miracles."** Power is synonymous with the Kingdom of God. If there is the absence of power in the life or ministry of an individual, it means that the Kingdom of God is not present there. This is because **"the Kingdom of God is not in word, but in power."** (1 Corinthians 4:20) No wonder the ministry of Jesus Christ was blessed with mighty signs and wonders.

As we look at some of the miracles, signs and wonders in the ministry of Jesus Christ, I want you to also see yourself manifesting or experiencing these things in your life because Jesus said in Mark 16:17,18, "**And these signs shall follow them that believe; In my name shall they cast out devils; they shall speak with new tongues; They shall take up serpents; and if they drink any deadly thing, it shall not hurt them; they shall lay hands on the sick, and they shall recover.**" If you will believe, you will certainly experience it.

The Blind Healed

The Bible mentioned seven blind men who were healed by Jesus Christ. These obviously were not the only blind people that were healed because Matthew 15:30 said, "**And great multitudes came unto him, having with them those that were lame, blind, dumb, maimed, and many others, and cast them down at Jesus' feet; and he healed them:**" Many other blind people were healed but only these ones were recorded to show forth Christ's mighty power.

The Two Blind Men in Galilee

After Jesus raised up the dead child of the ruler of the synagogue back to life, the Bible gave the account of what happened next as two blind men followed him. In Matthew 9:27-30, the Bible said, "**And when Jesus departed thence, two blind men followed him, crying, and saying, Thou son of David, have mercy on us. And when he was come into the house, the blind men came** to him: and Jesus saith unto them, Believe ye that I am able to do this? They said unto him, Yea, Lord. Then touched he their eyes, saying, According to your faith be it unto you. And their eyes were opened; and Jesus straitly charged them, saying, See that no man know it.**" Jesus did not turn these two men down, but rather, he had compassion on them and healed then of their blindness. He always healed those that came to him for healing.

Blind Bartimaeus Healed

The story of blind Bartimaeus is a popular and inspiring story of a man who was dogged and resilient till he got his miracle. He persisted till he got the attention of Jesus Christ, and the Lord being merciful, healed him and restored his sight. Mark 10:46 said, "**And they came to Jericho: and as he went out of Jericho with his disciples and a great number of people, blind Bartimaeus, the son of Timaeus, sat by the highway side begging.**" You can read the account of what happened here in Mark 10:47-52, "**And when he heard that it was Jesus of Nazareth, he began to cry out, and say, Jesus, thou son of David, have mercy on me. And many charged him that he should hold his peace: but he cried the more a great deal, Thou son of David, have mercy on me. And Jesus stood still, and commanded him to be called. And they call the blind man, saying unto him, be of good comfort,** rise; he calleth thee. And he, casting away his garment, rose, and came to Jesus. And Jesus answered and said unto him, what wilt thou that I should do unto thee? The blind man said unto him, Lord, that I might receive my sight. And Jesus said unto him, Go thy way; thy faith hath made thee whole. And immediately he received his sight, and followed Jesus in the way."** The Bible said that **"whosoever shall call upon the name of the Lord shall be saved."** Bartimaeus called upon Christ, and he received his sight.

In all the accounts of the blind men that Jesus healed, some came to him, others were brought to him, and he went to others, but in everything, he healed them. Even today, he still heals the blind.

Calmed the Sea and Walked On the Sea

Commanding the seas to obey him is one of the notable miracles in the ministry of Jesus Christ. In the account in Matthew 8:23-26, the Bible said, **"And when he was entered into a ship, his disciples followed him. And, behold, there arose a great tempest in the sea, insomuch that the ship was covered with the waves: but he was asleep. And his disciples came to him, and awoke him, saying, Lord, save us: we perish. And he saith unto them, Why are ye fearful, O ye of little faith? Then he arose, and rebuked the winds and the sea; and there was a great calm."** Jesus Christ is Lord over everything, and in your life, he is very ready to calm every storm, physical and spiritual storm.

The miracle of walking in the sea defiles every known physical law, as he exercised his authority over nature.

Devils Cast Out

In the ministry of Jesus, the Bible gave account of people who are possessed by evil spirits delivered. Matthew 8:16 said, "**When the even was come, they brought unto him many that were possessed with devils: and he cast out the spirits with his word, and healed all that were sick:**" There are many accounts of devils being cast out. Notable among them is the story of the man who had the legion In Mark 5:2-9, the Bible said, "**And when he was come out of the ship, immediately there met him out of the tombs a man with an unclean spirit, Who had his dwelling among the tombs; and no man could bind him, no, not with chains: Because that he had been often bound with fetters and chains, and the chains had been plucked asunder by him, and the fetters broken in pieces: neither could any man tame him. And always, night and day, he was in the mountains, and in the tombs, crying, and cutting himself with stones. But when he saw Jesus afar off, he ran and worshipped him, And cried with a loud voice, and said, what have I to do with thee, Jesus, thou Son of the most high God? I adjure thee by God, that thou torment me not. For**

he said unto him, Come out of the man, thou unclean spirit. And he asked him, what is thy name? And he answered, saying, my name is Legion: for we are many."
At the end of it all, the evil spirits came out of him.

In all account, No evil spirit was able to withstand the power of Jesus Christ. They just have to obey and come out.

Dead Raised To Life

Christ Jesus has the power to even raise those who are dead back to life. This is because death does not exist in the Kingdom of God. In John 11:43, 44, Jesus Christ raised Lazarus who had been dead and buried for four days back to life. The Bible said, "**And when he thus had spoken, he cried with a loud voice, Lazarus, come forth. And he that was dead came forth, bound hand and foot with grave clothes: and his face was bound about with a napkin. Jesus saith unto them, Loose him, and let him go.**" There is power over death in this Kingdom because according to Romans 8:2, "**...the law of the Spirit of life in Christ Jesus hath made me free from the law of sin and death.**"

All these miracles and many more than Jesus did are to show us that in the Kingdom of God, there is power over sickness, Satan, and death.

You Too Can Receive Your Miracle

The Kingdom of God is still capable of doing miracles because "**Jesus Christ is the same yesterday, and today,**

and forever." (Hebrews 13:8). If you are sick, he can heal you. If you are oppressed by anything, he can deliver you and set you free. Healing is the children's bread. Just as God did in days gone by, he is still doing mighty signs and wonders today.

THE WORK OF THE KINGDOM

> "I must work the works of him that sent me, while it is day: the night cometh, when no man can work." - John 9:4

In the Kingdom of God, God expects every citizen to work. Just as in an earthly Kingdom, the citizens have three responsibilities to fulfill which may include paying of tax, etc. When citizens fulfill their responsibilities, it will make the Kingdom bigger, stronger, and healthier.

Citizens of the Kingdom of God are not exempted from working. Every citizen is demanded and expected to work. Those who fail to work will have no reward on the final day when they will be judged according to their works.

There Is Work In the Kingdom

During the ministry of Jesus, he emphasized that there was work for him to do. He said in John 9:4, **"I must work the works of him that sent me, while it is day: the night cometh, when no man can work."** To emphasize the importance of this work, he said "**I must**". This shows that there is no option of whether to do the work or not. Everyone is commanded and expected to work. Jesus also said in John 4:34 **"...My meat is to do the will of Him that sent me, and to finish His work."** He was not just looking to start the work, but was aiming to finish it. This tells us that the work in the Kingdom is not seasonal, optional, or selective; it is an imperative and a commandment that must be obeyed.

Nobody can say that he or she is exempted from the Kingdom work. The work is given to everyone, both young and old. In Mark 13:34, the Bible said, "**For the Son of man is as a man taking a far journey, who left his house, and gave authority to his servants, and to every man his work, and commanded the porter to watch.**" You must always remember that you are a servant of Jesus Christ, and as his servant, anything that he commands you to do, you ought to do. The Bible said that "**he gave every man his work**". Nobody can deny that he or she was not given any work. The question is, *"have you discovered the work that was committed into your hand?"* It is important that one discovers the work that he or she is to do, and thereafter, dedicate him or herself to finish it.

In another place in Luke 19:13, the Bible said, "**And he called his ten servants, and delivered them ten pounds, and said unto them, Occupy till I come.**" The emphasis here is that "**he called his servants**". It is only the servants of Jesus Christ that are expected to do this work. People who are not his servants cannot and are not expected to do this work. Moreover, people who claim to be his servants but fail to do this work are not obedient servants. Every citizen of the Kingdom is called to the Kingdom work. This work is until Christ the King of the Kingdom returns. It is not a seasonal work, but a lifetime work.

> *Nobody can deny that he or she was not given any work.*

What then is this Kingdom work that we are to do?

The Great Commission

The Kingdom work is the greatest work in this world. It is called the Great Commission. It is greater than our secular work or religious activity. I said *"religious activity"* because one can be very active in the church, but very inactive when it comes to this great commission. What then is this great commission?

In Mark 16:15 the Bible said, "**And he said unto them, Go ye into all the world, and preach the Gospel to every creature.**" This was the risen Lord, Jesus Christ giving his disciples and to all the citizens of his Kingdom the final charge before his departure into a far country, into heaven. It is a charge and a commandment to "**go**" "**into all the world preach the Gospel**" This was what Jesus Christ himself did while he lived here on earth.

The Bible said in Matthew 9:35, "**And Jesus went about all the cities and villages, teaching in their synagogues, and preaching the Gospel of the Kingdom, and healing every sickness and every disease among the people.**" He went into all the cities and villages in his "world" preaching the Gospel of the Kingdom. He wasn't telling the people he went to preach to, stories, neither was he discussing politics with them. He preached only the Gospel of the Kingdom. What then is the Gospel of the Kingdom?

The Gospel of the Kingdom

The Gospel of the Kingdom centers on the life, death, and resurrection of Jesus Christ for the redemption of mankind. In 1 Corinthians 15:1, 3, 4, the Bible said,

> "Moreover, brethren, I declare unto you the gospel which I preached unto you, which also ye have received, and wherein ye stand; For I delivered unto you first of all that which I also received, how that Christ died for our sins according to the scriptures; And that he was buried, and that he rose again the third day according to the scriptures:"

Preaching anything more or less than this, is not the Gospel of the Kingdom. The Gospel is to emphasis the love of God for humanity that made him to send Jesus Christ who came and died for the salvation of mankind.

In John 3:16, we are expressly told that **"For God so loved the world that he gave his only begotten Son, that whosoever believeth in him should not perish, but have everlasting life."**

This is the Gospel that Jesus Christ commissioned us to go and preach. It is not a Gospel of condemnation, but a Gospel of redemption. It is also not a Gospel of hatred, but a Gospel of love. In preaching this Gospel, the aim is to bring the sinner to the cross where Jesus died for man's redemption, and to see that such an individual becomes a new creature.

As the citizens of the Kingdom go about preaching the Gospel that they have been commissioned to do, there are various steps and actions that must be taken if the preaching is to be effective. They include the following:

Preach Purposefully: As you go about preaching the Gospel, preach with a purpose in mind, the purpose that the sinner is converted and yearns for the Kingdom.

Preach Persuasively: When you are preaching, you are not to look like you are tired, not coordinated, and unable to persuade the person that you are preaching to. Preach in a way that will persuade the person to take action.

Preach Passionately: There must be passion in your heart as you preach the Gospel. You should not be lackadaisical neither should you be lukewarm. You should be passionate about the Gospel that you are preaching.

Preach Prayerfully: As you preach the Gospel, you should also endeavor to pray and seek for divine help. This is because there are forces of darkness that we are to contend with, and we can only be able to overcome them when we pray to God for help.

Preach Pungently: Your preaching should be sharp and must not shy away from calling the people to repentance. Preach with a sense of urgency.

Preach Persistently: You might preach to people today and they will not listen to you. You are not to run away from preaching, but must go back and preach again to them. Your preaching should be "in season and out of season".

We are called to occupy till Christ comes, to preach the Gospel to every creature, the watch and do the work of God. When we do these things, there are rewards that await us in heaven. This is the more reason why everyone must do the work of the Kingdom.

There Is Reward for Every Work Done

In the parable of the talents in Matthew 25: 14-30, Jesus told the parable of the servants who were given talents to use and trade. At the return of the master, the servants who worked with what was given to them received a reward, but the one who did no work was punished and cast out into prison. This parable was to tell us that there is reward for every work that we do in the Kingdom. As Paul the Apostle was coming to the end of his ministry, he said:

> 2 Timothy 4:6-8, "For I am now ready to be offered, and the time of my departure is at hand. I have fought a good fight, I have finished my course, and I have kept the faith: Henceforth there is laid up for me a crown of righteousness, which the Lord, the righteous judge, shall give me at that day: and not to me only, but unto all them also that love his appearing."

There will be crowns for those who did the work of the Kingdom. These crowns will be filled with many stars, and they will shine as lights. In Daniel 12:3, the Bible said, **"And they that be wise shall shine as the brightness of the firmament; and they that turn many to righteousness as the stars for ever and ever."** This rewards are prophetic, but before then, there are earthly rewards for those who do the Kingdom work.

In John 15:16, Jesus said, **"Ye have not chosen me, but I have chosen you, and ordained you, that ye should**

go and bring forth fruit, and that your fruit should remain: that whatsoever ye shall ask of the Father in my name, he may give it you."

This means that when we preach the Gospel and bear fruit in it, we can ask God for anything in prayer, and he will do it. This is a blank check that is only given to those who do the work of the Kingdom.

Think about the miracles you will receive, the open doors you will experience, the breakthroughs you will encounter, the joy in heaven for a soul that was saved through your preaching, the crown on the final day, and go and preach the Gospel of the Kingdom. Remember the finals words of Jesus Christ in Matthew 28:19, 20 saying,

> "Go ye therefore, and teach all nations, baptizing them in the name of the Father, and of the Son, and of the Holy Ghost: Teaching them to observe all things whatsoever I have commanded you: and, lo, I am with you always, even unto the end of the world. Amen."

This is the greatest of every commission. As citizens of the Kingdom, you must not fail to carry out this great responsibility that has been committed into your hands.

Chapter Reflections

1. _____
   _____

2. _____
   _____

3. _____
   _____

Segment Three

Deliverance

Chapter Eleven

The Foundation Of Deliverance

> "And it shall come to pass, that whosoever shall call on the name of the LORD shall be delivered: for in mount Zion and in Jerusalem shall be deliverance, as the LORD hath said, and in the remnant whom the LORD shall call."
>
> – Joel 2:32

The Word of God carries power. We release the power of God when we pray the Word of God. When there is an issue about a particular area of your life, locate the Word of God that talks about it, and release the power of God through the Word.

The World Corrupted By the Devil

Sometimes, the limitations we have come from the strategy and schemes of the enemy. Our archenemy is Satan. The Bible calls him our adversary. He is a deceiver and liar from the beginning. He was in heaven as Lucifer the son of the morning, and he wanted to rebel against the Lord. He became full of pride and was able to deceive one third of heaven angels. Then, God ordered Archangel Michael to cast him out of heaven. The Bible said,

> "And He said to them, "I saw Satan fall like lightning from heaven." (Luke 10:18 NKJV)

The contention of Satan for the soul of man started since the beginning of man. God created man to express his image and represent His governance upon the face of the earth. His intentions are to extend His power through man. Therefore, He put man inside the garden, but the devil came and brought man out of it.

Then there was need for salvation and deliverance. There is need for deliverance in our lives, families, workplace, community and nation. There was no need for deliverance until humankind entered bondage.

Let us look at the Genesis of man. The Bible says,

> "Then God said, "Let Us make man in Our image, according to Our likeness; let them have dominion over the fish of the sea, over the birds of the air, and over the cattle, over all the earth and over every creeping thing that creeps on the earth." So God created man in His own image; in the image of God He created him; male and female He created them. Then God blessed them, and God said to them, "Be fruitful and multiply; fill the earth and subdue it; have dominion over the fish of the sea, over the birds of the air, and over every living thing that moves on the earth." (Genesis 1:26-28 NKJV)

God blessed man. The word 'blessed' means empowered to prosper. We have authority from God to prosper. We are made in His image and likeness; we need to be empowered to prosper just as He prospers. Prosperity is not limited to financial blessings. I know a lot of messages and books talk about this subject, but I want to add that God gives greater blessings and His blessings are complete.

The word 'prosperity' comes from the root word 'shalom'. This is why Jews say that to each other. Shalom means fullness, completeness of all of life. It means the blessing of God covers your life, health, family, finances and future. It covers all you need for life and Godliness; all you need to be fulfilled and to live a balanced and complete life. This is what God intends for us. When you look at the world today, you see destruction of lives and communities by cocaine, marijuana, nicotine and alcohol; you see sickness, diseases, oppression, suppression and depression. The world today is far away from the reality God intends, and that is why Jesus came and died. He bridged the gap with the cross.

The Redemption Plan

God is still in the business of bridging the gaps, and this is where deliverance comes in. When you are far from the life God intends for you, then there is an activity of darkness limiting you. The devil still goes about operating to prevent believers from living life to the fullest. They are not seeing the fullness of what God has called them to be. They are not walking in dominion, despite being in the image and likeness of God.

We need to come into the full image and likeness of God. We need to be delivered from the corruption of flesh so that our life, personality and character may portray Christ. This is why we fast to deny self. Fasting is potent to bring about deliverance. The Bible says "**Therefore, just as through one man sin entered the world, and death through sin, and thus death spread to all men, because all sinned...**" (Romans 5:12 NKJV)

Through one man, sin and its consequences came into the generation of man. We can trace the lineage of every family to Adam. The devil planned to steal what God wants to do through our lives, to take us away from being the image and likeness of God. Adam did not struggle to be the image of God. Before he was corrupted, his very life totally expressed God's image. He spoke, acted and walked like Jesus.

When we come into the light of redemption, the first package we are exposed to is salvation. After this is deliverance. There is also the baptism into the power of the Holy Spirit. Then we begin to live like Christ every day. This is deliverance taking place in our Spirit and the salvation of our soul.

Then, deliverance deals with the body. There is tendency that from time to time, things will try to attack our body. However, we must take authority over sicknesses and diseases. The Bible says,

> "And these signs will follow those who believe: In My name they will cast out demons; they will speak with new tongues; they will take up serpents; and if they drink anything deadly, it will by no means hurt them; they will lay hands on the sick, and they will recover."
> (Mark 16:17-18 NKJV)

We must take our stand in God to contend for our destiny. We must take authority and fight the enemy from encroaching our families, home and the church. The things that people should have dominion over are dominating people's lives. People go into prostitution, drugs, selling guns, homosexuality, and all that, because of money. Money should not have dominion over you. Do not trade your dominion for money.

People sacrifice their divine assignments and move to corporate careers because of money. They sacrifice their relationship with God on the altar of money. A blessed man or woman is not dominated by money.

The Bible says,

> "Then God blessed them, and God said to them, "Be fruitful and multiply; fill the earth and subdue it; have dominion over the fish of the sea, over the birds of the air, and over every living thing that moves on the earth."
> (Genesis 1:28 NKJV)

God blessed them. He blessed humankind. The blessing was not just for Adam and Eve, but also as many that shall be born through them. He blessed you. Inability to live the blessed life is a curse. Do you know why?

The Bible says,

> "Christ has redeemed us from the curse of the law, having become a curse for us (for it is written, "Cursed is everyone who hangs on a tree")" (Galatians 3:13 NKJV)

Jesus Christ redeemed us from the curse of the law and the curse of the fall of man. To live below God's expectations is to be in curse. There are certain things that should happen to you by default because of your realization of the truth of the things God has done for you through Christ.

Life Outside Christ Is Miserable

Poverty, sickness and confusion are features of a life outside of God's scope, of blessing and grace. Such life is a cursed life. Our hope is not in what Christ is yet to do, but what He has achieved through the cross.

The issue is everyone wants to be productive but they do not know how. Everyone has the desire to walk in the fullness of life, and this is why when people do not live up to these expectations, they feel like failures. We preach the Gospel, not just for the salvation of people, but also for the blessedness of living life to the fullest. The blood of Jesus can break every curse off from your life.

If you stay faithful, your life can become the testimony of a transformed life. Wherever we are, we know that our blessing is not tied to what we do, but who we are in Christ. In the workplace, we are not weary or discouraged; we know that God is a rewarder of the diligent.

Once you stay with God, He will lead you until you locate your blessings. All you need do is focus on the words of God and not man. You do not have to look around; you only need to fix your gaze on Jesus. God's blessing is a process, and not an event. The more you stay with Him and align with His will for your life, the more blessings you access in Christ.

> "Then God blessed them, and God said to them, "Be fruitful and multiply; fill the earth and subdue it; have dominion over the fish of the sea, over the birds of the air, and over every living thing that moves on the earth."
> (Genesis 1:28 NKJV)

You are called to be fruitful and to multiply. Whatever God has given you has the potential to multiply, it all depends on you. To access the multiplication of God's blessings, you also need to increase your service to God and invest more in your relationship with God.

Inability to do this is a stronghold by the enemy to prevent us from making progress. You need to search the Word of God to know those things that are freely given to you by God for your victory. You need to know what resources and support system are in place and available for you to live the dominion and blessed life. The Word of God is very important; it can open you up to great wisdom that no one can offer you.

The Word of God can make you wiser than the wisest surgeon in the world can. This will make you smarter than it will make the greatest economist. This will make you wiser than it will make the greatest professor. The word of God is the food you should crave for daily. The Holy Spirit inspires the Holy Word of God. The word of God is the intention of God. The Word of God is the will of God. The Word of God is the perspective of God. The word of God gives access to blessings. When you learn the Word, it gives you authority to walk with great confidence.

Those who know their God shall be strong and do exploits. Anytime you read the Word of God, you have a revelation of who God is, and this strengthens and delivers you from ignorance. Stand strong and build your confidence in God's Word.

Jesus Brings Deliverance

The Bible gave an account in Matthew chapter 12 of what happened when Jesus brought deliverance in the life of people. It said,

"Then one was brought to Him who was demon-possessed, blind and mute; and He healed him, so that the blind and mute man both spoke and saw. And all the multitudes were amazed and said, "Could this be the Son of David?" Now when the Pharisees heard it they said, "This fellow does not cast out demons except by Beelzebub, the ruler of the demons." But Jesus knew their thoughts, and said to them: "Every kingdom divided against itself is brought to desolation, and every city or house divided against itself will not stand. If Satan casts out Satan, he is divided against himself. How then will his kingdom stand? And if I cast out demons by Beelzebub, by whom do your sons cast them out? Therefore they shall be your judges. But if I cast out demons by the Spirit of God, surely the kingdom of God has come upon you. Or how can one enter a strong man's house and plunder his goods, unless he first binds the strong man? And then he will plunder his house. He who is not with Me is against Me, and he who does not gather with Me scatters abroad. "Therefore I say to you, every sin and blasphemy will be forgiven men, but the blasphemy against the Spirit will not be forgiven men. Anyone who speaks a word against the Son of Man, it will be forgiven him; but whoever speaks against the Holy Spirit, it will not be forgiven him, either in this age or in the age to come." (Matthew 12:22-32 NKJV)

Jesus Christ is the one who has great authority and power over sickness and diseases, and He has power to raise the dead. There is need for the church to locate our inheritance in Christ again when it comes to healing. Diseases and sicknesses are satanic strategy and demonic assignments. In some cases, diseases are caused by specific demonic attacks on the body. The different ways of demonic attack is by possession, oppression or suppression. There is the spirit of infirmity, and we read that Jesus casted it out many times.

In verse 22 above, they brought one who was demon-possessed, who was blind and mute. He delivered and healed him. There are people who do not believe in the deliverance doctrine. While they seem to have a theological basis for their conviction, they cannot deny that Jesus delivered people from the influence of demons. The Bible says,

> "Then Jesus said to them, "When you lift up the Son of Man, then you will know that I am He, and that I do nothing of Myself; but as My Father taught Me, I speak these things. And He who sent Me is with Me. The Father has not left Me alone, for I always do those things that please Him." As He spoke these words, many believed in Him. Then Jesus said to those Jews who believed Him, "If you abide in My word, you are My disciples indeed. And you shall know the truth, and the truth shall make you free." They answered

Him, "We are Abraham's descendants, and have never been in bondage to anyone. How can you say, 'You will be made free'?" (John 8:28-33 NKJV)

The people Jesus was addressing here were also in the wrong frame of mind. They taught they did not need to be set free because they are free from the perspective of being of Abraham's descents. However, Jesus communicated the need to be free. Deliverance is when someone was lost and overruled by demonic strongholds and is set free; blind but now see; sick, but now healed, bound but now free; perverted, but now free.

There is no Kingdom that can stand in division. If you cast out Satan by Satan, then how shall his Kingdom stand?

If people are being delivered from possession, oppression and suppression of the devil then be sure that the Kingdom of God is the sponsor for such power. From the passage above, the Bible says,

> "Therefore they shall be your judges. But if I cast out demons by the Spirit of God, surely the kingdom of God has come upon you."

If you judge and attest that the power of God can deliver, then know surely that the Kingdom of God has come upon you. Demons are also called devils. They were part of the one third of fallen angels that were cast down from heaven.

We Can Cast Out Demons

The Kingdom of darkness operates a very organized system of leadership and operation.

The Bible says,

> "Finally, my brethren, be strong in the Lord and in the power of His might. Put on the whole armor of God that you may be able to stand against the wiles of the devil. For we do not wrestle against flesh and blood, but against principalities, against powers, against the rulers of the darkness of this age, against spiritual hosts of wickedness in the heavenly places. Therefore take up the whole armor of God that you may be able to withstand in the evil day, and having done all, to stand." (Ephesians 6:10-13 NKJV)

They are the principalities, powers, rulers of darkness and the spiritual hosts of wickedness in high places. Then, like the royal family, there is the prince, kings, queens, etc. The Bible talks of the Prince of Persia. They all exist in different levels and rankings, and are often housed in people.

The peace we have today is not because of lack of disturbance or trouble, but because God who watches over us does not sleep or slumber. The enemy seeks for ways to entangle or ensnare the believer constantly. He seems to have believers open their lives for attacks through sin or disobedience to God and His word, so that he can bring destruction and cause them to go to hell.

You do not have to be afraid of demons. They have no power over you. Part of your heritage is that you can cast out demons in Christ's name (Mark 16:17). It is part of the signs that follow your belief in God. You are covered and protected by the blood of Jesus.

> The Bible says, "For though we walk in the flesh, we do not war according to the flesh. For the weapons of our warfare are not carnal but mighty in God for pulling down strongholds, casting down arguments and every high thing that exalts itself against the knowledge of God, bringing every thought into captivity to the obedience of Christ, and being ready to punish all disobedience when your obedience is fulfilled." (2 Corinthians 10:3-6 NKJV)

You have your weapons of warfare. Your weapons are mighty in God. There is blessing in deliverance, and we must position ourselves to be vessels through which God delivers His people from whatever bondage they are in. In the Old Testament much of the weapon of warfare were physical. However, due to the spiritual position we now have in Christ and the indwelling of the Holy Spirit. Our battle now can sometimes be physical. But without a doubt battles ultimately emerge from a spiritual nature in which we have power over.

> The Bible says, "The Spirit of the Lord is upon Me, because He has anointed Me to preach the gospel to the poor; He has sent Me to heal the brokenhearted, to proclaim liberty to the captives and recovery of sight to the blind, to set at liberty those who are oppressed; to proclaim the acceptable year of the Lord." (Luke 4:18-19 NKJV)

We are anointed to heal the brokenhearted, proclaim and declare liberty to the captives (those in bondages), recover the sights of the blinds, set the oppressed free and proclaim the salvation of Christ. We cannot fulfill the scriptures in part and expect the whole blessing come to us. So Jesus said when you see these things happen, know that the Kingdom of God has come. How can we know the Kingdom of God? The Bible says, **"For the Kingdom of God is not in word but in power"** (1 Corinthians 4:20 NKJV)

It is good that many people are talking about the Kingdom of God. It is good that lots of teachings, messages and books are out there to talk about the Kingdom of God. However, it is time to manifest the power of the

Kingdom, because the Kingdom of God is not in word but in power. It is time to demonstrate the Kingdom of God. It is time for people to see the power of God through healing and deliverance.

The word of God said, **"... how can one enter a strong man's house and plunder his goods, unless he first binds the strong man?"** (Matthew 12:29 NKJV) Jesus used this earthly parable to talk about spiritual principle. You need to bind the devil if you want to deliver a man from demonic influence. You need to learn to rebuke and bind him.

The Bible says, **"The thief does not come except to steal, and to kill, and to destroy. I have come that they may have life, and that they may have it more abundantly."** (John 10:10 NKJV)

Prayer is very important to have deliverance. Prayer is a spiritual weapon, and when you begin to pray, you paralyze the devil. When you pray the word of God, faith rises in your heart. The Bible says, **"So then faith comes by hearing, and hearing by the word of God."** (Romans 10:17 NKJV) It also said that **"For the word of God is living and powerful, and sharper than any two-edged sword, piercing even to the division of soul and spirit, and of joints and marrow, and is a discerner of the thoughts and intents of the heart."** (Hebrews 4:12 NKJV) Another place says, **"In the beginning was the**

Word, and the Word was with God, and the Word was God." (John 1:1 NKJV)

Faith comes by hearing, and the hearing the Word of God. The Word of God is sharper than two-edged sword, and this same Word of God is Jesus. The Word of God is God's power in the world.

Fasting is also very important to having deliverance. Certain things in your life can only answer to fasting and prayer. Fasting causes your body to come under the subjection of the holy silence. It breaks up the power of flesh, and cleanses the mind and body. Fasting creates a suitable body and atmosphere for the Holy Spirit to move in you.

Always remember the promises of God in the following scriptures:

> "No weapon formed against you shall prosper, and every tongue which rises against you in judgment you shall condemn. This is the heritage of the servants of the Lord, and their righteousness is from Me," says the Lord."
>
> (Isaiah 54:17 NKJV)

> "Let this mind be in you which was also in Christ Jesus, who, being in the form of God, did not consider it robbery to be equal with God, but made Himself of no reputation, taking the form of a bondservant, and coming in the likeness of

men. And being found in appearance as a man, He humbled Himself and became obedient to the point of death, even the death of the cross. Therefore God also has highly exalted Him and given Him the name which is above every name, that at the name of Jesus every knee should bow, of those in heaven, and of those on earth, and of those under the earth, and that every tongue should confess that Jesus Christ is Lord, to the glory of God the Father." (Philippians 2:5-11 NKJV)

"Nor is there salvation in any other, for there is no other name under heaven given among men by which we must be saved." (Acts 4:12 NKJV)

When you pray, you need to engage the word of God with faith. Stand on the word of God with unshaken faith. One thing you should know is that Jesus has conquered already; you only need to validate His victory by believing. You also need to rest assure that your prayers are answered. We believe that when we pray by faith, our prayers touch God, and He honors His words. God honors our hearts and our relationship with Him, being children of God. We do not pray to God as though we speak to a strange deity, but to our Father, One who is touched with the feelings of our infirmity.

Every day, walk in the newness of life with the assurance of God's promises over your life. Every day, rise to plead the blood over your life, family, home, children, work, finances and assignments. Plead the blood over your health, and every part of your body. In Christ, victory is certain.

DELIVERANCE THROUGH THE BLOOD OF JESUS

Atonement in the Old Testament was achieved by shedding the blood of pigeons, turtledoves, and anything that the law required of. The animal is killed, its blood is sprinkled on men, sometimes poured on the altar, and that continued over and over again; as long as the priest and the people would appear before God's tabernacle.

Whenever a person touches anything that has made him or her unclean, the fellow is expected to go through the process of rituals, shedding the blood of a required animal in order to get cleansed. A leper in that testament is declared unclean, and cannot be allowed to live or fellowship with other people in order not to stain their cleanliness, hence, if a leper then get cleansed, he would still have to go through another purification process before he can be declared cleansed– according to the word of God.

The process of sanctification by the blood was continuous in that testament. This means that blood must be shed anytime anyone wants to go through the process of purification; the sacrifice of previous days would not be able to atone for another day, and there was an order that must be strictly followed for the sacrificed to be acceptable before God.

But then, before the world began, there was this lamb that was slain, He is called The Lamb of God. That scenario had been known by revelation, and then, it was translated into prophecies. His existence existed in the expectations of men for many years. Generation after, the arrival of the Messiah continued to be in expectation. And so it came to pass, the astrologers saw a sign in the sky; it was a sign of a newly born king. They had studied about His coming, they had anticipated it for many years. They knew that the star they saw was different from every other stars that they had ever seen. They couldn't hide their feelings, they had to travel down to the place where His star led them, and when they found Him; they worshipped Him.

Herod the King, at the time, was very cruel. He did everything in his capacity to have Him killed before His time. It was never written of Him that He would die as a baby, so, His blood could not be shed, and He was taken out of the land to a place considered safe at that time.

There was nothing heard about Him after He was taken to the temple as a baby. At 12 He was seen again in the picture discussing scriptures with the Scribes and Pharisees in Jerusalem. He was known as the son of a carpenter, for that was the profession of his earthly father; Joseph.

John the Baptist arrived before Him, to prepare the way for Him. Seeing the wonders of John the Baptist, the men of that time thought he was the Messiah. But then, John made them to understand that there was one coming after Him greater than him; in fact, he revealed to them that the Messiah was already amongst them.

When the day of His showing came, He approached John at Jordan, He was baptized, the Holy Ghost came upon Him, and He began to do great wonders amongst them. They wanted Him to be King, they thought the prophecy said He was going to be an earthly King. Actual, He was to already an eternal King, but before that would happen, a ceremonial ritual must take place.

That same kind of ritual that existed in the days of their fathers and even in their days (for they were living according to the Law of Moses) needed to be carried out, but this time, the sacrificial lamb was The Lamb of God. They seemed not to understand the mysteries of the prophecies that they had been reading for many years. They knew He was to become King, but they thought it was over Israel. They knew that His Kingdom was said to be so full of peace, because He is the Prince of Peace. They found it difficult to believe the mystery of His death and resurrection. Even Peter, one of His very good disciples tried to silence Him when He declared that He was going to die and be buried for three days. Nobody really understood why He had to die, until He had given up His life on the Cross of Calvary.

If the enemy had known why He was going to die, he wouldn't have allowed Him to die. If the devil knew that it was for his demotion, he would have done everything possible to prevent Him from dying. The enemy thought that by framing Him up and destroying Him, he would be able to stop Him from doing the good works on earth. Jesus was like a threat to him on earth. Yet, Jesus was not like the ordinary humankind that he (the devil) have overruled. He was always going around setting the people that the enemy had caged free. He was always preaching hope to the hopeless; strengthening the faith of everyone that had a contact with Him. The devil thought that His death on the cross was the end of His existence, he didn't known that it was going to launch Him into a new existence.

He was not killed by men, He gave up His life for the liberation of mankind. And as His life was being given up, His blood flowed down from His body, standing as a sign of atonement for all men.

The blood of Jesus works wonders. It brings to us deliverance from sickness, illness, infirmities and other diseases of the Egyptians. Isaiah 53:5 "But he was wounded for our transgressions, he was bruised for our iniquities: the chastisement of our peace was upon him; and with his stripes we are healed." By virtue of the power in the blood of Jesus, we are rest assured of victory over the enemy. No matter what anyone might be going through, there is power in the blood of Jesus to overcome. Certain people had been told in the past that they have issues in their bloodline. No matter what had been said about your bloodline, the blood of Jesus is able to purify and cleanse you; His blood is able to make you completely whole.

By virtue of the blood of Jesus, we have the assurance of the following;

- The blood gives us the identity that we bear in Christ as a righteousness of God and an Ecclesia of His presence.

- The blood of Jesus has and have given us power of all. We have strength over any form of weakness, deliverance from sin, victory over battles, healing over sickness.

- The blood of Jesus is a shield over those that believe in Christ and also do His bidding.

The blood of Jesus is capable of cleansing even the blood of any other person. If there be any curse, any kind of guilt, any dominance of fear, whatsoever it might be, the blood of Jesus is able to overcome them all. The blood of Jesus is without any blemish, unlike the blood of any other being.

Characteristics of the Blood of Jesus

- The blood of Jesus has victory
- The blood of Jesus has strengths
- The blood of Jesus gives hope
- The blood of Jesus gives power
- The blood of Jesus washes us clean
- The blood of Jesus has power to shield
- The blood of Jesus speaks on our account
- The blood of Jesus makes whole
- The blood of Jesus empowers
- The blood of Jesus purchases our salvation
- The blood of Jesus births the church
- The blood of Jesus makes the difference
- The blood of Jesus makes whole again
- The blood of Jesus is the bridge away from the old to the new
- The blood of Jesus paid for all our sins

There is nothing that the blood of Jesus cannot win over! No matter how hard the situation can be, it is by virtue of the power in the blood that a sure victory is guaranteed.

Are you in the midst of any battle? Are your oppositions standing on the same soil with you or are they existing far above in this space? It is important to note that whatsoever is above the earth is not above you, except there is such a thing that is far above God. The good news is, there is nothing of such that is above God, as God is above everything that is in existence. It is by virtue of the blood of Jesus that you have a space in God. You are in God and God is in you, so, there is nothing of such that is above you. Therefore, whosoever or whatsoever represents the enemy cannot overcome you.

> Revelation 12:11; "And they overcame him by the blood of the Lamb, and by the word of their testimony; and they loved not their lives unto death".

Sometimes, the battle of some could be connected to their health. There are certain people who were born with certain infirmities, as it is traceable to their family-line. Some folks encountered health challenges while growing up. There are certain people who are currently battling with health issues that came as a result of sinful living. Whichever category anyone falls into, the blood of Jesus is able to heal and deliver.

There are so many people on the surface of the earth who are battling with their past. Many of us had got memories that we are still trying to get rid of. Many do not even feel qualified to call upon the name of the Lord, just as many had concluded in their heart that with the gravity of the things that they had done in the past, they are not so sure that God will ever be able to forgive them. The good news is still the same! It was because of you that

Jesus Christ chose to die. While on the cross, He gave His life in exchange for yours. It was because of that sinful past of yours that He shed His blood. By the power in the blood of Jesus, you possess the ability to overcome any form of condemnation that the enemy may be raising in your heart to fight against you or even physically. Glory to God! There is power in the blood of Jesus.

It is quite important to note, that every lost person is saved by faith in Christ's Blood.

"Being justified freely by his grace through the redemption that is in Christ Jesus: Whom God hath set forth to be a propitiation through faith in his blood..." Romans 3:24-25; "Propitiation" means "place of mercy." So, we have mercy from Christ "through faith in his blood."

In heaven, where God the judge of all is, and where Jesus, the mediator of the New Covenant is, there also is "the blood of sprinkling" (Hebrews 12:23, 24). The blood of Christ, which is subject to no corruption, is sufficient for us even to the end of the world, because the blood of Christ is always distilling before the presence of time. He entered once into the holy place; with this blood of the covenant he entered immediately upon the breathing out of His soul on the cross, into the holy of holies in heaven. One thing cannot be left out of our emphasis; the blood of Christ is the life of the Gospel. When we go into heaven itself we shall not have gone beyond the blood of sprinkling; we shall see it there more truly present than any other place.

What The Blood Does?

- Provides forgiveness of your sins. "The law requires that nearly everything be cleansed with blood, and without the shedding of blood there is no forgiveness." (Hebrews 9:22, NIV).

- It removes the power of sin over us. 1 John 1:7 (KJV); "But if we walk in the light, as he is in the light, we have fellowship one with another, and the blood of Jesus Christ his Son cleanseth us from all sin."

- Gives you life. "Then Jesus said to them, "Most assuredly, I say to you, unless you eat the flesh of the Son of Man and drink His blood, you have no life in you." (John 6:53)

- Brings you close to God. "But now in Christ Jesus you who once were far off have been brought near by the blood of Christ." (Ephesians 2:13)

- Cleanses your conscience. "How much more shall the blood of Christ, who through the eternal Spirit offered Himself without spot to God, cleanse your conscience from dead works to serve the living God?" (Hebrews 9:14)

- Gives you boldness to approach God. "Therefore, brethren, having boldness to enter the Holiest by the blood of Jesus…" (Hebrews 10:19)

- Sanctifies you. "Therefore Jesus also, that He might sanctify the people with His own blood, suffered outside the gate." (Hebrews 13:12)

- Cleanses you. "But if we walk in the light as He is in the light, we have fellowship with one another, and the blood of Jesus Christ His Son cleanses us from all sin." (1 John 1:7)

- Heals you. "He himself bore our sins in his body on the tree, so that we might die to sins and live for righteousness; by His wounds you have been healed." (1 Peter 2:24, NIV)

- Delivers you. The Blood of The Lamb brings deliverance from bondage, unproductivity and also helps in bringing about God's perfect plan for our lives.

- It gives you victory. Even after the Israelites had crossed the Red Sea the Pharaoh followed them until God drowned them, similarly the Blood of Jesus Christ grants us victory over the enemies that trail us because it is the enemies of the people who are covered by the Blood of the Lamb that God destroys. (Romans 12:19, Nahum 1:2, Deuteronomy 32:35)

- Cleansing and Purification. The Blood of Jesus Christ purifies us and only it can change our hearts and minds. Hebrews 9:13, 14 (KJV) "For if the blood of bulls and of goats, and the ashes of an heifer sprinkling the unclean, sanctifieth to the purifying of the flesh: How much more shall the blood of Christ, who through the eternal Spirit offered himself without spot to God, purge your conscience from dead works to serve the living God?" Matthew 5:8(KJV) "Blessed are the pure in heart: for they shall see God."

- Access to the Spiritual Realm. It is only through the Blood of Jesus Christ can we enter God's presence and it is evident through the below verses Hebrews 10:19(KJV) "Having therefore, brethren, boldness to enter into the holiest by the blood of Jesus" Ephesians 2:6(KJV) "And hath raised us up together, and made us sit together in heavenly places in Christ Jesus:" From all this we see the importance of the Blood of Jesus Christ and how necessary it is for us to apply it in our daily life.

- Enables you to overcome the devil and his works. "And they overcame him by the blood of the Lamb and by the word of their testimony..." (Revelation 12:11, NIV)

The Blood is Important

The Blood is so important to God that it is mentioned in the Bible around 700 times. David referred to it as the "incorruptible" blood. Peter spoke of the "precious" blood. And John wrote of the "overcoming" power of the blood. In Leviticus 17:11 that, "the life of the flesh is in the blood." This is true in both spiritual and physical realms.

Your natural blood supplies life-giving oxygen and nutrients to every cell in your body, as mentioned before. If the flow of blood were to be cut off from an area of your body, that part would begin to die. Spiritually speaking, any part of your life that is cut off from the blood of Jesus is dead or dying.

Your blood also carries away wastes and toxins from your cells. Spiritually, without the blood of Jesus, your life would be filled with filth just like the Pharisees in Matthew 23:27. Thank God for the blood of Jesus that removes the dirt of sin from our daily lives!

The Shed and the Sprinkled Blood

At the Last Supper, when Jesus held up the cup of wine, He said, "...This cup is the new covenant in my blood, which is shed for you" (Luke 22:20). The blood of Jesus is so significant that this scripture is used every time we receive communion. Still, most Christians know only about the blood being shed and not about it being applied.

In Exodus 12:22, the Israelites were commanded to kill a lamb and dip a branch of hyssop (a common herb) into its blood.

The shedding of blood was not enough – the blood only had saved them when it was taken out of the basin and applied!

God Looks At the Blood

It's important to note that God's protection wasn't dependent on the zeal of the Israelites or their good works. He wasn't looking at the degree of their morality or even their devotional habits. God was looking only at the blood, and He is still looking only at the blood!

Throughout the Old Testament, it was the blood of sacrificed animals that had the power to atone or make amends for wrong doing. We read about this in Leviticus 17:11, where it says: "For the life of the flesh is in the blood, and I have given it to you upon the altar to make atonement for your souls; for it is the blood that makes atonement for the soul."

However, in the New Testament, Jesus said, "This is My blood of the covenant, which is poured out for many for the forgiveness of sins" (Matthew 26:28, NIV). Even though there is nothing any person can do to compensate for their sins, many keep trying to make up for the things they've done. It may be something big or small: an addiction, an affair, an abortion, an angry outburst, an unforgiving heart – but the blood of Jesus is the only thing that can bring about the forgiveness you and I need.

In 1 John 1:7-9 we're told, "If we walk in the light as He is in the light, we have fellowship with one another, and the blood of Jesus Christ His Son cleanses us from all sin. If we say that we have no sin, we deceive ourselves, and the truth is not in us. If we confess our sins, He is faithful and just to forgive us our sins and to cleanse us from all unrighteousness." When we admit our sins to God, the blood of Jesus provides complete forgiveness and cleansing.

Without the blood of Jesus, we are defenseless against the devil and his works. Yes, it's good to have zeal and do good works. It's good to have a high degree of morality and a strong devotional life. But none of those things alone can cleanse, heal, or protect you. When it comes to your forgiveness and cleansing, your healing, protection, and deliverance, God is still looking at the blood!

The Blood

Just as the blood had to be sprinkled on the doorposts, you also must apply the blood of Jesus. It was already shed for you, but it becomes powerful in your life when you apply it.

Under the old covenant, the blood of animals was applied by sprinkling with the hyssop. Under the new covenant, we apply the blood of Jesus with our words.

"For with the heart one believes unto righteousness, and with the mouth confession is made unto salvation" (Romans 10:10). You apply the blood of Jesus when you say, "the blood of Jesus was shed on the cross for me."

You can apply the blood of Jesus to receive healing (Isaiah 53:5). You can apply it to protect your household (Exodus 12:13). It can be applied to cover your children and their circumstances (Job 1:5). You can apply the blood to anything you have authority over or influence upon. And whatever you apply the blood of Jesus to becomes redeemed by Christ, and Satan cannot touch it.

His Blood in Your Veins

When you were born, you were born in sin. You carried the sinful nature, doing things that you didn't even want to do. Some of the things that seems natural to you are not right, yet, those who are still fully living in the natural still find themselves fulfilling the lust of the flesh, at the detriment of their precious soul.

One thing that cannot be left out of our emphasis is that, Jesus did not only come to shed His blood that it might flow on the ground or by Faith cleanse us from iniquity; the blood has also been shed that we might begin to live by its dictates.

If truly "the life of a being is in its blood", then, it is not erroneous to say that as believers, we are able to connect the life of Jesus through His blood. This justifies the scripture that states that "the life that we currently live is not ours but it is the life of God that is at work in us"(Galatians 2:20).

If the blood of Jesus Christ is going to be effective in your life, then you must be willing to accept His life. Who is he that can accept a new life, without doing away with the old life? You must die to self before you can be alive in Christ.

The blood of Jesus Christ is able to save, heal and deliver, hence, it must also be the source of your existence.

- Can the blood of Jesus be infected by any sickness or disease? Never!

- Can the blood of Jesus be successfully attacked by devils and evil spirits? They dare not!

- Can the blood of Jesus be flowing in a man and he so desire to sin without any control over self? Not at all!

- Can the blood of Jesus be flowing in you and you don't love God? No way!

- Can the blood of Jesus be the Source of your life and you lack passion for the Kingdom of God? Not at all!

If truly that blood has saved you from all iniquities, if you know that through faith in the blood of Jesus Christ you are free from the guilt of past deeds, if you truly have the understanding that through the blood you are cleansed from all forms of sickness and diseases, then, it must also enter your consciousness that through the blood, you have the life of God flowing in you– you are free from sin and shame.

Hallelujah! Praise God! You are a new creature! You have not just been saved from sin and sicknesses, you can also represent God on the land of the living. Just as Jesus is the Light, you are also the light of the world. The Holy Ghost is only able to dwell in you because you have the blood of Jesus Christ at work in your life. When God looks at your bloodline, it is not that corruptible blood that he sees but the blood of His dear Son.

Any church where the blood of Jesus is not duly emphasized is not on track. The Blood of Jesus Christ, is the reason for our living; the reason of our gathering. Any church or religious organization that does not accept what Jesus has done and believed that He is the only, the truth and the life, and That He is Lord is not of the true and living God, but rather a cult.

Chapter Reflections

1. _____
   _____

2. _____
   _____

3. _____
   _____

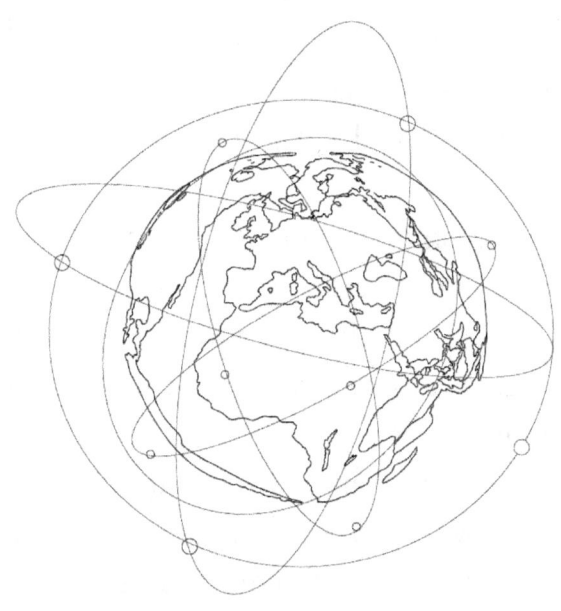

Chapter Twelve

Religion Versus The Kingdom Of Jesus Christ

Religion has held more people captive than anything else; whether it is the satanic religion, the religion of men or the philosophies and doctrine of men or devils. It has held people paralyzed. There are about 7 billion people on the earth and sadly, religion has held more than half captive.

Many are worshipping idols and many are worshipping dead gods and material things. If Satan sees that he cannot get to you by making you worship idols, he can destroy you by bringing you into a false doctrine; the doctrine of men.

Does it really make sense to worship something that you created as your God? For instance, a carving or a self-image that you created of one's self. The Fact is you created it, you can change or image or change the carving or redo and undo the God. You see, the creator has more power than what is created. But our Lord is unchangeable.

> "But seek ye first the Kingdom of God and its righteousness; and all these things shall be added to unto you
> (Matthew 6:33).

These days' men have been seeking after religion, after church, after theology (the study of God). Jesus wants you to seek first the Kingdom of God but sadly, almost everyone is seeking after religion. But Jesus wants you to study the message of the Kingdom. The first requirement is the Kingdom of God.

The Kingdom Of God?

Jesus will return with a new heaven and a new earth. Until then, he has sent the Holy Spirit into the hearts of every believer. The bible says whosoever believes in him shall have eternal life.

No other gospel, no other religion produces that. The Gospel has changed men who were once wife beaters to successful businessmen. The Gospel brings a great things from a life that you would have written off. No other Gospel or doctrine takes men who are depressed and hopeless and gives them hope and gives them eternal life thorough Jesus Christ. Do you know how I know that the Kingdom of God is real? The Kingdom of God makes a whole family of the entire nations. No other religion on the earth unifies people. However, there has been a great deception that is crafted.

The Study of Religion

In the Bible, Paul who was formerly called Saul, was a Pharisee and a persecutor of the Christian. He was a religious man in his time. He was a teacher. However, he thought it right based on religion to persecute and to kill every family he could come across preaching the Gospel of Christ. This man was ambitious but he was only following after his religion and so killed for that religion.

But this Saul had an encounter with Jesus Christ; Jesus confronted him face to face. He showed up himself with a supernatural power to Saul. Saul fell blind and had to be led for a few days to a house where a man prayed for him where the scales and the blindness fell off his eyes. This Saul, who later became Paul, studied and followed Jesus Christ passionately and he is the one who travelled around most of that known world and transformed it. He began to teach, preach and declare the Kingdom of God with power around the world.

So Paul began to study; you know as skilled as he was in the Law and the Prophets, it was also easy for him to study about Jesus and the Kingdom of God. He wrote at least 13 of the New Testament books.

Darkness relates to Satan; Satan has a Kingdom which is of darkness and his assignment is to kill, steal and destroy in the lives of many people. Satan is ravaging the lives of many people using a lot of vices; alcohol, drugs, sexual perversion depression, generational curses, and so on. When you accept Jesus Christ you can be delivered from the power of darkness which only has failure, suicide, depression, torments and the like to offer you.

Knowing Where You Belong

There is the Kingdom of darkness where Satan is lord but Jesus has his own Kingdom and it is the Kingdom of light. We have been bought with a price and the price is the blood of Jesus. Jesus knows that you do not have the power to overcome Satan by your own self. So he through his own blood redeemed us.

The minute you came out of your mothers' womb, you were born a sinner. From Adam's fall throughout all the generations before you, you were born a sinner. Which is why we have the Gospel of Jesus; we have a savior. Who made all things? All things were created by Jesus; all things in heaven and in earth. Whether, they were principalities or powers or people, all things were created for him (John chapter one). Jesus made Lucifer, the storms and the waters and the floods.

Some of you are afraid of Satan. Jesus made Lucifer who later became Satan. When you say the name of Jesus come out, your command have to be obeyed, because Jesus is the one who made them. Jesus is also the head of the body; referring to the Church. He made the Evangelists, the Apostles, the Pastors, etc. For some churches, Jesus is their head, while for some churches; they have kicked him out as the head.

Remember that when Jesus came into the earth, he was the father in flesh (John 10:30). Some religion has it that the father and Jesus are separate. They say that the Father is one Person and Jesus is the Son and another Person. Some say Jesus is the Archangel Michael. Many say that if it is not the father then it is not God. Further, many say that it is idolatry to worship Jesus as the Son. Not worshiping Jesus; they do not praise Jesus. They see Jesus as being separate from God which is not so. Do not be deceived by such things. Take some time to read the book of John and the book of Colossians for yourself. Further the book of Revelation expresses all the Glory, honor and Power that was given to Christ because of His obedience.

MAN – WORSHIPPING

Man is being worshipped that is why there is no power. People carry the words of their Bishop more than the words of Jesus Christ. Some people cannot even tell you what the word of God says, but they can brag about the church they go to and what the prophet says. It is becoming idolatry, witchcraft and it is called man worshipping. There are those who give "Prophets" all their money because they want to hear what they have to say but do not know what God has to say.

Some people are standing on the false prophetic word that was sent to them. Some people are standing on false promises, false doctrines which has caused them to be accursed (Galatians 1:8).

The Religion of Man and the Worship of God

God had just delivered the children of Israel out of Egypt where they had many gods. Note also that the Lord used everything that the Egyptian worshipped to destroy them. They worshipped Frogs; he sent frogs to afflict them. Do you know that there are people who worship the Sun and the Moon, etc.?

Some nations worship the moon; some religions' symbol is the moon. Horoscope is the worship of the moon and the stars. People worship the zodiac signs; the signs of the stars. Some base their business deals by the signs of the stars. They place their marriage by the signs of the stars. Break this power of the zodiac signs over your life; stop reading horoscopes. Stop calculating your life on the strongman of the zodiac sign.

There are pastors who are using such to deceive people. They get their prophecies from the calculation of such signs and numbers. They use numerology and add up numbers to deceive people. You do not need that; you need Jesus. Many people still use the dream box to interpret their dreams. But God is saying: *"I give interpretation of dreams with my spirit and not with the use of any dream box".* Get Jesus!

He will show you what he wants you to know through his word. God gives his instructions that you are supposed to follow. He tells you what to do. But since you cannot even obey the Word, you cannot get deep revelations from the word that you are reading. The Gospel is so simple. Some of you do not even know where Joshua is in the Bible; cannot quote 20 scriptures in the Bible. You have to learn more of Jesus first.

There is so much divination around; the use of spells, using all kinds of enchantments. In every country, we have many different kinds of witchcraft. But in all witchcraft the devil is behind it. They try to interpret dreams, interpret visions. They try to look into your eyes and tell you things that they can see, they look at your palm also. Some persons even take your money and do divination on it.

That is why some people cannot keep their husbands (because they got him through witchcraft and have to keep him with witchcraft). Whatever you get through the occult, you have to keep it with occult. Yoga is also witchcraft; and there is no such thing as Christian yoga.

Yoga is the worship of Hindu religion. Karate is from Buddhism. It is alleged that Buddha went to Indian where the Hinduism religion came from. From this came Buddhism. Nowadays, we have Pastors who are deep into Karate. Many people who do karate are bound; they have a strongman in their lives. You cannot serve God and serve Karate. Take not that the Karate moves emulate animals. We have also seen Christians practicing Yoga. Some of them do not eat meat. We mean they see eating meat as a sin. Jesus ate meat. During the Passover, they used to sacrifice a lamb and eat it and Jesus partook in the Passover. Be careful of some of these practices and the spirit behind them. It comes from or is border line Hinduism, where they don't eat certain meats because they believe that one reincarnate as that particular animal etc.

Some culture and some nation dedicate their food to their gods. They feed their food to their gods. And for you that does yoga, do you know that all their postures are dedicated to their Hinduism? Further, all these dances, moves and twerking are demonic.

Do you know witches uses mind power to control people? People use their mind to control things; they project it and control it. Parents, there are young people going to the internet searching for such occult power. They are looking for occult power.

- If you give money to people to pray for you, it is witchcraft.
- If you burn incense, that is witchcraft.
- If you put special candles, all is witchcraft. Charmers are also witchcraft.
- Some people have demonic rings and demonic necklaces. It is also witchcraft.

Not everyone who prophesies is under the influence of the Holy Spirit; some of them are consulting familiar spirit. They deal with the forces of darkness. Some of these pastors, have gone to meet the devil for powers. We have heard personal accounts where Apostles, Prophets, Pastors, Teachers and Evangelist (5-Fold Leaders) etc. confess that they went demonic agents to get powers. In many cases because of the Corona virus shut down all over the word, many are not falling for them works– and so they have lost a lot of money and wealth.

Before then when they pray for someone and such prayers were being answered, or they speak that something will happen it actually happens. Do not be deceived! It is not the Spirit of God; it is consultation with familiar spirits. Some people like food, some like money and those are some of the things that pulls people into witchcraft. They use such things to entice people and get them into sorcery. Some even use free material to entice.

Do not be too desperate for anything; the enemy could use that to bring you into the demonic powers.

Do not be deceived either; prophets are not called to maintain your life. They should only say what God wants them to say when He wants. Pastors and preachers should build people up in the word for long term, so stop running after prophets, pastors and preachers.

All of the Lord's ministers should speak God's word in the name of Jesus. Not everyone who preaches on television are actually real men of God, it just means that Satan gave them more audience. Just because someone has a lot of followers' does not mean that it is the truth. Islam has 2 Billion followers but it does not mean that it is the truth. Jehovah's witnesses has millions of people; it does not mean that it is the truth. So don't get alarmed by numbers. Always look for the truth. Every prophetic words should be the testimony of Jesus (Revelation 19:10). In other words, it should lead one to Jesus. We have seen where persons are given prophetic words (Who is known to live an ungodly life) and it does not come to pass. It was just a word that appeased the flesh and seeking after materialism.

In Deuteronomy chapter 18 verses18 to 22, God is saying that if you prophesy without him authorizing you, you will have to die. God is saying that if you presume and you are talking without him telling you to, you have a great punishment waiting for you. When you change the word of God, God says that you are worse than your fathers. The church keeps changing the word, they keep changing the word so they can bring a little of the world into the church. And then one begins to say, it doesn't matter anymore. And so the church is no longer different from the world. The church is not supposed to change the Gospel to suit the world; to suit sin. Rather, the church should influence and change the world.

Nothing else is as wonderful as knowing Jesus personally. Do away with any religion of men and seek to know and follow after Christ.

Chapter Reflections

1. _____
   _____

2. _____
   _____

3. _____
   _____

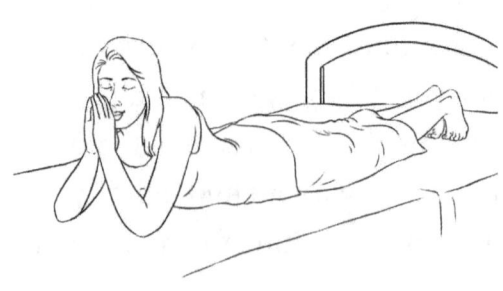

Chapter Thirteen

The Kingdom Of God Versus The Kingdom Of Darkness

The enemy has so many tactics; he wants to kill, steal and destroy. But where did this war started from? Why are we talking about this? I feel that this is a time when we need to reset some of the thoughts that we have had. Some of you are going through storms and some of you are going through crisis which the Lord is going to reset. This is a time to reset. Things that you have planned and prepared will be reset.

When you reset your life, you reset it on the foundation of the word of God. The word of God will reset your life. When we decided to reset on the word of God; we decided to go into the word of God and reset everything that we knew, understood and walked in prior to. We had to reset everything; you also have to reset your life.

This is a time to reset. When you reset your life, it means some of your abilities that were being destroyed and have been locked down, have to start on a new foundation. Now, a new foundation has to be laid. And that is what we are going to be doing; we are going to be re-laying a new foundation on the word of God.

There is spiritual warfare and some people do not believe that. Some church does not want to talk about spiritual warfare. For most persons growing up, they are just in church thinking that there's no demons or devils. However it is true that they, there is a Kingdom of darkness. I have been in the deliverance ministry for years and I have seen spiritual warfare and demonic deliverance. I know spiritual warfare because I have seen it with my own eyes so there's no doubt about it. That which is in the spirit is more real than that which we see and experience now. Science will tell you that there are more things that are invisible to the naked eye than are more real. There is more to what these physical eyes can see. Science will tell you there are neutrons, atomic particles that are so small that you cannot see with a naked eye but it is real. There are so many things beyond our understanding because the world and the universe is so vast. In deliverance we have heard demons tell of their assignment to destroy a person's life, whether by suicide, sexual perversion etc. We have commanded the demons to come out with a cry or screaming and kicking in Jesus' name and it was so. If a demon resisted and had the person violent or coiled up. We have asked angels to straighten out the hand and feet in Jesus' name and it was so. Right before our very eyes. I have seen persons healed form specific demons that had them bound such as schizophrenia and different pain about the body in Jesus' name.

> On a particular occasion a minister attended a service complaining of pain in the spine and having an appointment to do back surgery. Upon ministering deliverance we discovered that the oppression came upon her life from an outfit and jewelry that was given her through a third party form a particular region.

> "And there was war in heaven: Michael and his angels fought against the dragon; and the dragon fought and his angels, and prevailed not; neither was their place found anymore in heaven. And the great dragon was cast out, that old serpent, called the Devil, and Satan, which deceiveth the whole world: he was cast out into the earth, and his angels were cast out with him. And I heard a loud voice in saying in heaven saying, now is come salvation and strength and the kingdom of God and the power of his Christ, for the accuser of our brethren is cast down, which accused them before our God day and night" (Revelation 12: 7 – 10 KJV).

The book of Revelation just talked about a real war, and let me tell you, you are in a war. Every human being is under the attack of the enemy. There was a war in heaven; you and I are in a war. This war is bigger than us; it is a war between God and Satan. But our Lord and God have already won the victory.

How do I know that? Well, Michael and his team fought against the dragon (Satan). Jesus sent his war angel to fight him and they fought against the dragon and his angels. So Satan also had angels. Satan fought with Michael and was kicked out of heaven.

A BRIEF HISTORY ABOUT THE DRAGON

Satan may be ugly now, but the Bible described in Ezekiel 28 verses 12 – 14 that when he was created by God, he was in the Eden (Eden was the presence and the spot where the Glory of God was). Satan was in the actual presence of the Glory of God and then his body was full of precious stones. His body was a musical instrument. So when they show these ugly pictures of the devil, I do not think that is how he actually was. In Ezekiel 28, he was in heaven and was a beautiful angel.

> Further, the devil will not appear today in all cases as some ugly creature if he wants to snatch your soul, killing, stealing and destroying you. He can also appear as an angel of light and use

demonic agents. Such as a man you destroys a woman's destiny and vice versa or a woman who destroy another woman. A woman may pose as a dear, caring friend just to turn the woman into a lesbian lover. Or with friends who leads one astray to commit crimes, getting locked up etc. There are so many possibilities. You would need the gift of discerning of spirits to discover who people and things really are about.

Satan was a covering spirit. He was an angel that was in the glory of God, very beautiful. He was an anointed cherub angel that covered. He was in the fiery presence of God and he walked in the presence of the almighty God. We are seeing this because we have to understand our adversary. He had beautiful pipes in his body which is why he could make such beautiful music. And today, we see that music is one of the greatest tactics that the enemy uses to deceive the nations.

Do you know when his problem started? It started when the Bible said that he was caught up in his beauty and lifted himself in his pride. I am telling you today that if you have pride, you have the spirit of Lucifer, if you have the spirit of arrogance and you feel that you are better and greater than others, you have the spirit of Satan. The spirit of rebellion is also the spirit of Lucifer.

Now let us get back to Revelation chapter 12 verses 7. He was Lucifer in heaven, and beautiful in Ezekiel 28 verses 12. Revelation 12 talks about what happened in the beginning. Michael then fought against him and his angels. Then the bible says that Satan took one - third of the angels with him (this can be found in revelation 12: 4) and then they became demons.

You have got to understand that this is real and not a fairytale. Demons and devils are real. They've been real before the foundation, after the foundation of the world and the earth. And he is continuing that, he wants to destroy you. So when he was kicked down from heaven, he was now known as what? The great dragon! Any time, I see dragons promoted as a symbol in any form, the martial arts, the creative arts and they promote the dragon; they are promoting the symbol of Satan. You know why? You do not see Jesus being described as a dragon but instead Satan is known as a dragon and a serpent. Any time you think about a snake or a serpent, most people in any part of the world have an apprehension with snakes. Only some people like snake charmers love snakes. He is known as the old serpent called the devil.

He is also known as the deceiver of the whole world. There are people using Facebook or all these social media platforms claiming to talk about Jesus Christ. Paul talk about another gospel and another Jesus. It is not the Jesus who we know died, was crucified, buried and rose again on the third day by power of his blood. In our deliverance session we have also discovered on a few occasion a demon called "another Jesus" or "False Jesus." The Gospel that those ones are sharing is a new Gospel; a watered down version; a new age thinking and there is some mixture of different occultism beliefs which is the work of Satan. If the devil sees that he cannot keep you away from Jesus Christ, we will try to pervert the gospel that you hear. Many preachers, prophets, ministers etc. out there sometimes never once mention Jesus in their presentation. That is why you have to get this word for yourself. Or you have to be under an anointing message like this one.

> Once we decided to test the songs that were playing on a Christian Radio Stations. For over three hours the songs playing basically were about things that a person could from God. Not one song within a two hour period mentioned Jesus or Glorify God for who He is. Instead, it was centered on man and what they can get or appeased to the spirit of the flesh of men.

The devil wants to deceive a lot of people right now, there is witchcraft and deception being used and there are people that are being used and sucked dry. And I found out that so many people like deception, they liked to be around people who are deceiving them and abusing them, robbing them and taking from them. Satan, your enemy is a deceiver according to the Book of Revelation. The enemy's job is to deceive the whole world and he will continue to do it. He was cast unto the earth and his angels were cast down with him.

Another thing with Satan is that he is an Accuser. He is the accuser and he will accuse you. How does he do it? He tells you how bad you are, how done you are, how defeated you are, how disgusting you are etc. He brings up your past to accuse you. The blood of Jesus is powerful, the blood of Jesus will clean, heal, deliver and set you free from anything but the enemy's plan is to keep you in accusation. Why? He wants to accuse you before God. He wants to call you a liar, a cheat, a whoremonger and a deceiver. He has people to accuse you; people in the church to accuse you, he has your family members to accuse you, people in your community to accuse you, people in your job accuse you, and people around you to accuse you. Wherever you see accusations, it is the work of the enemy.

One of the enemy's greatest tactics is to accuse you before God, accuse you before heaven, and accuse you before heaven and earth. He will accuse you because when you are under accusation, you cannot be what God wants you to be.

You keep thinking about the mess you have done. When God has forgiven you through the blood of Jesus, you do not have to keep beating yourself over it –and do not let people beat you over it. Get up and move on and do the work of God because once Satan can paralyze you, he will accuse you. The Kingdom of darkness wants to accuse you, which is why it is dark. He is an accuser; he wants to keep you in bondage of your past and in the bondage of your mistakes. Have you made mistakes? I am sure that many of us has made mistakes, and if I am to be counting my mistakes, I will not be where I am today. Praise the Lord that I rose up in the blood of Jesus. I received the blood to forgive, to heal and to cleanse me. I am free by the blood; I am whole by the blood.

What have you done? What have you said? What have you watched? What did you get involved in? The blood of Jesus is able to cleanse us. That is my point! So the Kingdom of darkness's job is to bury you in accusation and he uses the enemy to accuse you.

Now, if you are in sin and he is still accusing you, he has every legal right to do that. But, if you are out of that sin and you have turned away from it. You have repented to God and apologized to everyone who you have hurt and you have told God that you are turning and you are changing, the devil has no right to accuse you.

> "And they overcame him by the blood of the Lamb, and the word of their testimony; and they loved not their lives unto death" (Revelation 12: 11).

What does this mean? You can overcome the Kingdom of darkness through the blood of Jesus. You cannot do it without the blood. The only thing you need to know today is that the blood of Jesus works. The blood of Jesus can wash away sin; the blood of Jesus can forgive and the blood of Jesus can make you whole.

Well who told you that the blood of Jesus cannot rebuke the enemy? It is the same invisible blood, the same powerful blood over 2000 years ago that was shed by the Jesus. The only person who is the Lamb of God, who was holy, and faithful and pure in heart and has received power.

Satan hates the blood of Jesus. He hates the undefiled blood. He hates the blood that heals, the blood that has no sin.

Who is the head of the Kingdom of darkness? It is Satan.

Who is the head of the kingdom of light? Jesus Christ.

Binding the strongman

Who is this strong man? The strongman is a body that operates under Satan's law. The word of God said, seek ye first the kingdom of God and His righteousness and all this things shall be added unto you. Jesus says my Kingdom is not of this world. Satan does not have time to be fighting every one of us but he has a complex system and kingdom that works; people, invisible beings and satanic powers.

I have been in the deliverance ministry for years and I have seen demons being cast out of people. Satan does not want people to know that he is real so he can dry up people. Also, some ministries try to avoid deliverance ministry because they do not want people to know about Satan and his tactics. They want people to think that they can just walk around saying they are doing great but where God wants them to be has to be greater and they have to bind the enemy to get to that next place.

You could do really well, you could have a wife. You could be gifted with a great job and a career and family and you could just live comfortably. But if you want to get into the greater things of God; if you want the mysteries of God unlocked in your life you have got to go to a great place in God. There is a greater assignment that is why you have been pushing to be greater, you do not want to be in the same place. You get tired of the routine work every week. There is something in you that should want more; more from your life, more from God. And all these while, there is an enemy that stands against you and you don't even know. When the Lord began to open

> *There is something in you that should want more.*

my eyes to see the things that he wants for me is greater than the things the enemy has placed. I began to recognize what those things are and I began to pray. I was released into things in my generation. Things in my bloodline, things my grandfather and grandmother and great grandmother were involved in; not knowing such things ignorantly. I began to tell God to show me and I began to break those curses and I was delivered and set free.

When I hear of people going for Halloween, I begin to pity them because they are ignorant of what they are doing. How can you go to Halloween? That's Satan's kingdom. When you go and sit there, you are opening up to Satan. When you put those things around your house, you are opening up to the spirit of Satan. When God opened my eyes to see these things, we began to pray that God should break any way we might have opened our lives to the enemy.

I saw Christians wearing witches and wizards outfit. When people do that, they are ignorant of the Devil's devices because he is going to bind some people up and cast them down as innocent as they seem. Satan is very real; we have enough warfare and we should not open up to anymore. If you are a believer, you should not put on witches and skeletons and bones and ghosts and demons.

Even as subtle as watching horror movies. I am not going to be a fan of the Devil. We were ignorant of it before.

A former witch told us that when we engage in that, we forfeit our purpose. That when we put those things in our doorway, we are saying Satan should come into our house. Those things are not unto Jesus, they are unto Satan. When you open up to the devil, he is going to afflict you with sickness and disease. And you know those things might not be revealed now, until one day when you are praying to God and he tells you that those things you opened up to, that food you ate are the devices of the enemy. Ask the Lord to purge you of any demonic food now, in Jesus 'name.

Satan has set up a strong man against your life. I have seen so many tactics that the enemy has done. Even before you were born, Satan was setting up your mother and father to curse them so that you will be born cursed. The Bible says that the Lord knows you from your mothers' womb he formed you in your mother's womb, do you not think that Satan and his demonic powers do not know you? The same way that you have angels assigned to you to bare you up when you dash your foot, Satan has given demons charge to come after you, to destroy you. He's a counterfeit of everything that the Lord does. When God said in his word that he knows the plan he thinks towards us, plan to bring us to an expected end is the same way that Satan has plans to steal, kill and destroy.

When the Lord says that by His stripes you are healed, Satan puts sickness and disease over your life.

The Kingdom of Darkness. Luke 11: 14

Jesus cast out devils; why then is the church afraid of casting out devils? Any ministry that believes in the power of God, this signs follows them. It did not say that these are the signs that shall follow them that should have an international ministry.

It did not say the signs that would follow that have a great television ministry. The first sign that I want to suggest is that you cast the devil out of people. Do not to feel bad about it because there are many people possessed by the devil living among us. Why is there no place for deliverance anymore? You can sit people down to be counseling them. You can give good advice to someone who is bound by the enemy but that is not what Jesus did. Jesus knew how to deal with it and I prefer to follow Jesus.

Deliverance; when we who are in the Kingdom of God confront the Kingdom of darkness. There are some deep things about your life deeper than you think. The enemy has strategically fallen into your life. The enemy had launched a specific attack to destroy your life even from when you were young. Some of you as teenagers, the enemy had set up a strategic attack upon your life. So, as it nearly destroyed your life. The same way God was protecting you because of the call of God upon your life, the enemy set up something to attack you.

Defeating the Enemy. Luke 11: 17

The first rule of warfare is that you cannot be divided. If you are a family and you are divided, the enemy already has a legal right to destroy you. ***Any Kingdom divided against itself is brought to desolation (Mar 3:24).*** If you are an owner of a business and your employees are fighting against you, you are going to fall automatically. Division brings automatic doorways to Satan's plans to destroy you without you even knowing. You can pray all you want but if your marriage is already separated, Satan has very little job effort left to destroy you. If your ministry are divided, if there are witches planted in your church or around you, you are going to be destroyed.

The first rule in being delivered from destruction is to bring in unity and order with everyone around you. There are some people that you might have to cut off because you are going for Jesus and their life is totally against it.

Jesus is saying that Satan's Kingdom is strong and I wish the church will be stronger. I wish the saints will be unified instead of fighting one another. Satan does not divide himself; his Kingdom cannot be divided. Satan's Kingdom is strategic. The Kingdom of Jesus Christ is the Kingdom of light and it is powerful. I am telling you that

Satan has infiltrated the church, he has infiltrated the body of Christ and he is infiltrating the believers. He is infiltrating many lives. His strategy is to bring division into our lives and the lives of those following Christ. Now the church of Jesus Christ is also bringing destruction to the Kingdom of darkness –deliverance. Those who understand the right and the power that they possess in Jesus Christ and the authority that they have in the name and the blood of Jesus are using it to bind up the enemy. It stop up Satan's work, stop his assignment.

The Kingdom of God is not in word but is in power; one of authority. Jesus said all powers have been given unto me and he has given that power, he has given the keys of the Kingdom to the church. And whatever we bind on earth is bound in heaven, and whatever we loose on earth is loosed in heaven. Do you know what this means?

It means that everything we need to do must be done in the spirit. That is why the enemy fights; he fights because he knows that when Jesus said that he has given us authority, he has given us power and victory in the heavens and over the devil.

We need to cast out and bind the enemy from our place in heavenly places. Because, right now, you are seated in heavenly places with faith and thorough the word of God. So you must pray from that position of the heavens. We are seated in heavenly places with Christ Jesus. We are crucified with him, and, "nevertheless I live but it is no longer I that live but Christ that lives in me" (Galatians 2:20). This is you also. If you have been crucified with Christ you have been raised to life in him so you have to reign with him. Do not pray with guilt, shame and condemnation in your heart anymore, you are to pray from a place of authority which is where you are.

If you have the Kingdom of God in your life, it means you must be at warfare. You must be a spiritual warrior, a spiritual child. You must do it through your warfare in prayer and with hands that war and fingers that fight (Psalm 144:1). You can lay hands on people, you can bind the strong man over your life and family, you can pray over your city. You have the authority so use it. You don't need a pulpit; some people do not need a pulpit to bring victory into their life and city. If you are in the Kingdom of God, you can deliver yourself, your city, your career and you can speak to nations around the world. Using the authority of Jesus Christ and the power that he has you can bring victory to people.

Why do I want you free? It is because there is a world that is dying and the Lord is raising a mighty army and he wants you there. He wants to bring deliverance and set people free. You have to be strong in your faith and your spirit because you are going to rescue people. You can rescue your friends, your family members, your coworkers etc., from the attack of the enemy. You cannot preach the gospel around you and people still go to hell, you have to preach this so as to deliver them. Pray for your family members; some of them have a strongmen in their lives who wants to destroy them, who wants to kill them. The Kingdom of God is marked by power and deliverance and breakthrough. There is no end to deliverance. Everyday work on deliverance. Deliver yourself every day from the grip of the enemy. When God shows you where the enemy is still tormenting you, use his blood and confess it and break the bounds of the enemy.

Do you know that the devil calls you his palace? He is a devil that does not want to let you go. Pray that Jesus comes as a stronger man and overcome the strong man in your life (Luke 11: 22). The enemy has an armor and so declare that the strong man should be stripped off his armor and devices in your life. The enemy uses this armor to protect himself from being attacked from you because he does not want to be defeated. He does not want to lose hold. There are so many people walking the earth today and they are occupied and filled with the evil spirits. They want to be set free, they are depressed, and oppressed, and suppressed. They are beaten and guilty and they feel worthless, and helpless. No matter what they do, they cannot be set free even though they love Jesus.

Pray for your family members.

The Lord is stronger than the strong man, he is the Lord of host and he wants his people set free. He wants the unfruitful works of darkness destroyed in your life; he wants to uproot the unclean spirit and drive them out of your life Let Him do it.

Some of you will claim that you have been delivered but the strong man came back and saw your life in place. He saw you clean, he saw you focused, and he saw you advancing. He saw your marriage intact, and he saw you walking in your destiny, then the bible says and ***...taketh to him seven other spirits more wicked than himself.... (Matthew 12:45)***

So that is eight spirits against your life. Do not play with the enemy because he is not playing with you. His job is to see that you do not reach your goal, for you not to get to your finishing point or accomplish anything.

The devil will allow you to get a house and a car and still bind you without a peace of mind. Some people have great cars and great houses but they want to be set free. They are in turmoil because they are bound by a strong man and seven other spirits and they want to be set free. They go to church after church, crusades to crusades because they want to be set free.

There is no end to deliverance.

Well you can just ask God to sanctify you, and bring you into the Kingdom of God, ask him for the blood to sanctify you and break the power of the deceiver in your life.

Bring deliverance into your life through the blood of Jesus today. You are going to be set free.

Chapter Reflections

1. _____

2. _____

3. _____

Chapter Fourteen

Disarming The Enemy

The bible says in Isaiah 40: 31 *that those that wait upon the Lord shall renew their strength.* The keyword that I want to use is "wait". The word wait is from the Hebrew word "Carva" which means those who have hope. I want to remind you that this is the time more than ever to anchor yourself to the word of God; in the scripture of God. If you also think of "wait" as in a waiter; serve the Lord.

The bible says heaven and earth will pass away, but my Word will never pass away and so people of God, for those who are going through physical storms, sometimes the only thing we have to hold on to is just the word of God. I want to encourage you that the word of God is the sword of God; never put down the sword of God at this hour. Anywhere you go, you have to take the sword with you.

Soldiers that go into the warfront take their weapons with them so you must always have your sword with you. These are the times that you have to use the word especially times when there is nobody else to call on. The word of God is always safe and secured. Those who are going through difficult circumstances, the word will always keep safe.

Jesus came down from heaven and he experienced the pain and so, some times when we go or have gone through things, we can also identify people who are also going through it. This is the time to call upon the name of the Lord.

Do you know why we need the Word of God? It is because if we do not get it together, to call and quote the word of God, the enemy will progress in our lives. He could open a doorway through what we see, what we hear, and what we say.

Sometimes, our hearts become corrupt, sometimes our heart becomes weak, and so we are not filled with the word of God. Even if it is one scripture you get and hold on to it, your faith will rise and it will put the enemy away. Be reminded of the Israelites, God came to them in the wilderness. They were warned that they should not store the manna till the next day, but that they should only pack what they would eat in a day. Some people still disobeyed and what did they get? What happened to the manna by the next day? It was spoilt and rotten.

You have to be careful at this time; you cannot lie and be deceitful because destruction will come your way.

You cannot allow the Glory of God come off you at this season.

The word of God is real and this is the time when the Lord is giving us wisdom to be on the offensive, to destroy the enemy. Sometimes the enemy re – strategizes; when our spirit is down or troubled the enemy is making more plans. You have to stand firm on the word of God.

You have to remember that the Lord is a consuming fire and keep saying that the Lord God will save you and if he does not save you he is still God (Just like the three Hebrews said in Daniel 3: 16 & 17).

The Lord has given us divine promises which enable us to share in his divine nature and in that way, we are in the world and not of the world.

I want to remind you of the reason why we have authority. You see what our Lord and Savior went through for us in Isaiah 53:12. He did that so that we could have victory, so that we could overcome, and so that the heart of our understanding might be open, he did so that the mystical things might not be hidden from us anymore. You need to destroy the strongman and everything that concerns him.

Let nothing separate you from the Lord; your God. Those who know their God shall be strong and do exploits and they are going to show their strength in the

Lord. It is when you know the word of God, that you are able to fight the devices of the enemy.

Our real enemy

We must understand that there is a real enemy and we must know how we are going to disarm the enemy. People will start asking: How are you going to do this? Are you not afraid to attack the enemy? One of the best time to fight against the enemy is when you are the strongest. When people go to the track for a race, they do not go when they are tired but they go when they are strongest.

Those basketball players do not just come out to play when they are weak, they come out in seasons strongest. They would have undergone a lot of training so that when they come out to play, they play their best. That is what you are doing now; you are learning how to fight the enemy.

Whether you believe it or not you have an enemy to fight. It does not have to do with you being a good person or not, or not wanting to fight. It does not even matter if you believe in warfare or not. What is real is here is that you have a spiritual enemy.

When you are a Christian, automatically the devil is after you so you will have to fight anyhow, and either way. You are not exempted from the fight; you are not exempted from this warfare. You are going to fight until you get back what the enemy has taken from you.

Binding the strongman

Well some of you might be asking, what is the strongman? I am glad you asked. Well for many years I walked in my Christian life but was getting beaten by the devil. I was ignorant of his powers; I was ignorant to warfare and deliverance.

If a country wants to go for an attack on another enemy nation, they spend months trying to study the enemy country. So that is what we are doing, we are training ourselves to know more about the enemy. So that when we fight, we do not fight on one level. The devil can come through the air, which is one of the levels he operates in. He has powers in the air, and in the second heavens. The strongman and demonic forces operates in the air and then come to operate on the earth to fight the church and the people of God.

Then we have under the sea, the marine spirit; the demons that operate in the underworld. When we go deeper, we say the realms of hell. In the earth, they also operate in the hearts and minds of people. So we are going to learn how to fight in every aspects. You have to deal with it in your mind, you have to deal with it in your body (in your flesh), and you have to deal with the problems that have been in the earth from your forefathers. You need to deal with the demons that is fighting you from the oceans and the sea. You need to bind the strongman in every one of those areas. Just as in the natural there is no different in the spiritual; in fact the spiritual world is more real than the physical world. You may have heard of mermaids, these things are nothing but marine demons. Marine demons affect many aspects of the lives of people who leave, near the sea, oceans rivers etc. One of the proven traits is that there is a lot of sexual perversion. You will see it in their clothing and even hair styles.

Matthew 12: 29, Jesus called a spirit demon a strongman; that is a real person. What do I mean by person? Demons are real personalities, they might not have physical bodies but they are real. The devil wants you; he wants to destroy you. What is his plan? His plan is to steal, kill and destroy and that is what he intends doing. So do not play with the strongman, do not play with the devil, do not play with demons, and do not play with the spirits of the enemy. He is nothing to play with. If you do not destroy him, he will destroy you. If you do not get rid of the strongman. The moment you identify the strongman and know that he is real, then he begins to shake in fear because he knows that he has been exposed.

Some common demons:

- Fear – fear of every and anything
- Lust – seducing, desire for sexual pleasures
- Defeat – cannot succeed at anything

- Death – Everything or your endeavors always die, or cease
- Generational curses – Could be anything from rape, incest, all the women having cancer, men dying at a certain age, no one gets married,
- Gambling, drinking, suicide, depression, female problems, abortion, unforgiveness, racism

Over 2000 years ago there were demons, and even today. Do you think that just anyone could kill a child? Do you think that just anyone could live a perverted lifestyle? They have a demon, they are possessed. Now when one who is a believer participates in those action they are said to be demonized. And all they need is to be willing for deliverance to take place.

If you talk to some people who are buried and addicted in pornography, they will tell you that they want to get off it. No one wants to be bound to shame.

If the word of God says that people are possessed, who are you to say people are not possessed. These murderers around, drug dealers, they are all possessed. At that time the Pharisees might have been religious but they got one thing right: they knew about casting out devils. They did not deny that the man had devils. So why is it that the church in this present age now say that they are no demons? How can there be demons 2000 years ago and there are no demons anymore? The Pharisees and the religious people acknowledged that the man was demon possessed, they acknowledged that the demon was casted out but the only thing that they did not acknowledge is that he cast them out by the Spirit of God. The word **Beelzebub** means **Lord of the Flies.** When you see a dead animal and you see those flies hovering over. Now what the Pharisee is saying is that Jesus is casting out demons by Beelzebub which is the Lord of the Flies; that is he is using the power of the chief demons. Beelzebub is really Satan. And Jesus answered them and said, any Kingdom that is divided against itself shall not stand.

And that is the first point: if your house is divided it shall be destroyed, if your marriage is divided it shall soon be desolate and so Satan does not need to destroy you, you destroy yourself. If anything pertaining to you is not in one accord, then it is ready for destruction, if you don't releasing to the Lord to restore it right away. Most people around already gave a doorway to Satan.

Some pray, without an action. You do not pray over demons, you cast them out. Some pray and say that they are not getting a breakthrough. What they need to do is to cast the devil out! Drive out, push out, get out, kick out those are the words you need to use for the devil. We pray and we drive out. When some people steal from you, sometimes you do not only allow them to just go without making them pay for it. Instead, they are charged to court which make them pay in some form or the other. In some cases when the thief learn of this they will return all what they stole from you. That is how you do it with prayer. You will not just allow the enemy to go scot – free, at times; you just need to take action against the devil.

Drive the devil out; use every avenue to drive the devil out. When Jesus casted the devil out, it was not with the power of Satan. Satan will never cast out demons from you. Instead he takes out your cold and replaces it with cancer afterwards. So do not go to voodoo, obeah or the occult for a cure. Satan might help you get that man; but that man will beat you left, right and center. He might help you get that woman but that woman will kill you. He might help you get that job promotion but he is coming for your life or your child's life. Once he takes a devil out of you, he will replace that one with 10 more devils.

Satan's Kingdom is not divided. He will send one person to you and you will think that you are doing a good deed, then he sets you up and before you know it you are done! Do not be ignorant of the devil's devices! There is a strongman that wants to kill you. If Jesus, who is the king of your life, says do not do something, and you continue to do it, are you not divided against him? And let me tell you, you are going to fall. God's Kingdom cannot fall. His Kingdom is unshakeable! Stay under His protection.

When demons are cast out, when there is a strongman and you fight against those principalities and powers you are advancing the Kingdom of God. This means that if you are not casting out demons, you are not advancing the Kingdom of God. So, whatever chance you get, keep binding the devil, in your home, in your family, in your career, in your future, in your environment. Keep binding the works of darkness, bind witchcraft, sorcery, divination, fornication, adultery, death, suicide, corruption, illness, fear, failure and all other unfruitful works of darkness.

You have the spiritual authority. You have part in the authority of Jesus Christ; you have authority in the realm of the spirit. You must begin to loose God's blessings, loose God's mercy, God's favor, God's provision, God's goodness, God's salvation and deliverance. Don't be a regular Christian at this point in your life. You better have some binding and losing power.

In Matthew 12: 29, Jesus now introduces the concept of strongman. How can one enter into a strongman's house? How can a man enter into a strongman's house and bind him up?

There is an enemy that does not want victory for God's people. When sinners who drink, go for parties and etc., before you know it they have children. Then two people who loves the Lord get married and then all hell breaks loose. They may struggle to have children. Before you know it they are struggling to keep their marriage together. The devil wants every generation under the strongman's power.

You do not have to be afraid of demons, and devils and evil spirits because, Jesus is the stronger man. Here are some powerful things you need to know about the strongman:

- The strongman is real
- The strongman has power
- The strongman has armors on
- The strongman guards his palace. (The palace of the strongman is your life)
- He keeps all of his goods in the spoil (He takes all your heavenly possessions and guards them so you will not get it. he prevents you from getting it).
- The strongman is an unclean spirit.
- The strongman walks about trying to get into a human life.
- The strongman talks.

Of course, Jesus would not have called him strong if he did not possess powers; so the strongman is powerful and he is armed. He is full of different weapons that he uses to get into the lives of the people. At times, you might be wondering what it is that is keeping your blessings, keeping your breakthrough, it is the work of the strongman. He keeps things that belong to you away from you and so you do not get to the desired position where you are meant to be.

Those listed points are there to help you understand the strongman better and to know what you are dealing with. You are not dealing with a mere man, but with principalities and powers and so do not keep allowing the strongman to oppress and take authority over you. You have been given authority; use it in to bind and take over the things that the strongman has taken possession of.

Identify the strongman and command it to lose its power. Begin to expose the unfruitful works of darkness. Evict him out of your life, drive him out, and chase him out. Tell the strongman to release your goods unto you; command him to release everything concerning you and disarm the strongman!

Chapter Reflections

1. _____

_____

2. _____

_____

3. _____

_____

Chapter Fifteen

The Strong Man And The Strong Powers In Your Life

Who is the *strong* man? It is a strong powerful force that is sent to attack; a demonic power who comes in to take possession of your life, your generation, your family, your finances and everything concerning you. It comes and works with seven more other powerful spirit to kill, steal and destroy and take captive of any person. You might feel that there is nothing against you; that you are just a good Christian. You go to church and you serve God and so the enemy is not against you.

Many people are tormented. Sometimes you just feel like there is something hindering you, something keeping you from progressing, something stopping you. That is an example of what we are talking about. That is the strong man!

The strong man operates through a legal ground; it could be through your generation, it could be through some of your past mistakes and some of the things that people did to you. It could be some associations that you are with, it could be through relationships that you are being part of. These things are what could be a legal ground for the strong man to operate in your life or torment you. If the enemy has been tormenting you or your family members, God is ready to save you from the tormentor.

There has been a war in heaven.

Revelation 12: 3 & 4 is talks about Lucifer and the war in heaven. And guess what happened, the enemy (Satan) called the great dragon took one - third of the host of heaven. This is how the stronghold began; this is how demonic forces started. An individual either belong to the Kingdom of God or the kingdom of darkness, there is no middle ground.

Do you know how many people are being terrorized by the enemy and they feel like they are just good people. They do not belong to the Kingdom of God. The enemy has a war against your life; do not think that he is going to let you go free, you must be merciless against the strong man and the seven spirits that work with him.

If you find that you cannot move forward, there is a strong man that you must dispossess. The bible in revelation chapter 12 verses 9 called the devil a great dragon, the old serpent, the deceiver and Satan. This is a real enemy and revelation chapter 12 has told us plainly who the enemy is. Satan's greatest tactic is to try to remain anonymous. He does not want you to know who he is and he does not want the people of God to know that he exists. He allows people to make fairytales about him so that people do not know his works among the people of God. He does not want people to know that he is oppressing them, killing them and destroying them.

In Matthew 12 verse 22, Jesus does a supernatural miracle, he heals and he delivered someone who was bound. People who have certain conditions are bound by the devil and the devil needs to be cast out of their lives. When I am talking about the devil, I am not talking about just one devil; I am talking about the one third of the host of heaven that was kicked out of heaven. The bible did not say anything about the actual number of the host of heaven, but it sure was going to be much and for the devil to take one third of the host of heaven with him. That is a lot of demonic forces and stronghold to fight against the people of God.

According to Matthew 12 verses 28 and 29 If Jesus referring to some force as strong it must be really strong. Because he is Lord and God of all, and we must take note of it.

Your life is called the house of God; the bible says that "**know ye not that you are the temple of God?** Which means that the strong man that Jesus is talking about is the demonic power that occupy, destroy you and hold you captive in your mind, captive in your body, captive in your spirit, and captive in your faith never fulfilling the counsel of God on your life. Now, the strongman does different things; he can overpower you, he binds you and takes away every good thing.

The strong man in your life could have been there from the time you were born. If you find that you cannot increase, in your life that could be a strong man. Look at your life, look at your family, and identify the strongman in your life. Begin to observe different things that occur to you at different points in life, you will begin to notice the presence of a strongman or a stronghold. Cancel that demonic power from operating in your life and in your generation.

There are some things in your family line which you inherited and we call it generational curses but those curses are the demonic power that does not want to let you go. I have seen this practically from deliverance, and from what I have seen during deliverance, these demonic powers start expressing themselves because they do not want to leave.

The strongman comes in through generation, then the strongman also comes in through your lifestyle. Many gave the enemy a doorway through their lifestyle. Such lifestyle could include addiction to alcohol, sex (masturbation, lesbianism, homosexuality, bestiality) etc.; you tried it and couldn't let go of it again. Even though you love Jesus, you are bound by these things and you cannot control. It is something that maybe ashamed of, and feels like you cannot escape from it; you cannot tell anyone either. These things overpower you, it overtakes you and no matter what you try to do, it feels like you can't let go, that is a strongman. You love Jesus but you are bound by bitterness, you love Jesus but you are bound by lies, you cannot seem to help yourself whenever you want to lie and whatever it takes, you lie continuously.

You love the Lord, and you worship and you pray but you cannot get out and you try everything to stop it. That is a strongman!

The strongman that comes with unforgiveness.

I want you to know that the strong man against your life; this demonic power that Jesus talks about is armed and dangerous. This is a strongman that is prepared to fight just like in Revelation chapter 12. Do not think the devil wants you free; do not think that he wants you delivered. Do not think that the devil will give up your life so you can walk in your destiny. No! You will have to rise up to fight for your peace, you will have to fight for your breakthrough, for your sanity. Fight to get free from that toxic relationships. You will have to fight to break the chains off. You will have to be strong but you do not have the strength. Jesus knows that you do not have the strength and that is why he said there needs to be a stronger man and that stronger man is Jesus.

Jesus said that "he that is not with me is against me" (Luke 11: 23). When you come to the Lord, and you surrender to the Lord, deliverance by accepting the Holy Spirit takes place. As you start to live Holy, as you study and as you pray, he begins to break such yokes in your life. Some people get saved and they never go through deliverance, I would not advise that. If you got saved, you need to be delivered from any strongman that was in charge and those things that you were involved it.

When the devil, demons and unclean spirits are driven out of your life, they come back seeking and when they find your life looking nice and clean, and your mind is together, you are worshipping and praying (they see you free from your addiction and your lifestyle), they come back with their deceit and before you know it you are back in their web again.

That is because the unclean spirit does not want to let you go; not because you got free last year means that you will be free this year, or that the enemy is not coming back for you. The enemy is always out on your case; that is why we need the full armor of the Lord. Put on the whole armor of God. This is why we need the blood of Jesus; we overcome by the blood of the lamb and the word of our testimony. The power of the word will keep us.

Some persons and many of their family members and people around are bound not only to the strong man

Put on the whole armor of God.

but to the seven other spirits that the strongman brings. And the last state of that man is worse than the first (Luke 11: 26). There are people who are bound by these eight different spirits and they need deliverance. You need to get them to know it. This strongman is wicked; he does not go out to get weaker spirit or just one. He goes out to get 7 seven more evil spirits more evil than the strongman himself. There is no need to play games with the enemy any longer because the enemy wants to destroy you and keep you bound.

In Matthew 18: 15 Jesus was saying that if you have someone who has offended you, you can go to them one or one and beg them for forgiveness. There are people who are working in deep torment because of unforgiveness, bitterness, anger and resentment.

When you are serving the Lord, there are some people that the enemy is going to send to say all manner of evil concerning you; people in the church who will say all kind of evil concerning you. You will have to forgive them and love them. Some of the things that people have said concerning you and what they did to you, you will have to forgive them. If not, the enemy is going to send a strongman of unforgiveness, bitterness and malice. Before you realize it, the strongman and seven other spirits are able to take over your mind.

When Jesus was saying you should forgive, he was only trying to prevent the strongman from wrecking into your mind. When Peter went to Jesus to ask him how many times he should forgive his brother, Jesus said 70 X 7 times. Now, 70 X 7 times is 490 times. How many of you have been able to forgive a person 490 times?

How does unforgiveness comes about? When you love deeply and you get hurt deeply. You are almost sure to be faced with unforgiveness. But if you do not let go of the hurt and the pain, you can still be tormented by the strongman. Some people's heart is already cold and they are bitter, they are full of gall and jealousy and every unclean spirit that comes through the spirit of unforgiveness. Jesus is saying that he is going to hand you over to the tormentors. Jesus said if you do not forgive, his father in heaven is going to hand you over to the tormentors to torment your life. If you are not still willing to forgive you better do so. You are not doing it for them; you are doing good for yourself. The tormentors do want to destroy you.

You do it because you want to break the curse of the tormentors waiting to destroy your life. The tormentor wants to destroy your life and stop the blessing of God upon your life.

Some of you have lack, and is it of the devil, yes it is of the devil but he has legal right with the tormentors to steal, kill and destroy. What did the enemy kill, steal and destroy? Some of you it could be your peace of mind, your sleep, some of you cannot find joy, you cannot find restoration. You know why? It is because you are bound by unforgiveness. No matter what anyone has done to you, you should forgive, no matter the pain and the hurt that you feel, you should let go and forgive. If Jesus could forgive your sins and your trespasses, you should be able to forgive others that have hurt you.

Jesus said do not allow the sun go down on your wrath. If we forgive a lot of things will be saved. Some of you go to bed angry and by in the morning you wake up with such demonic dreams. You better forgive and don't bring it up or the enemy will torment you. Science is saying that if you harbor anger or unresolved anger in your life, it is possible to have some diseases. Bitterness could cause depression, heart failure. When you refuse to forgive, there comes tension in your body.

Judgment and the strongman

Many people are under the judgment hand of the Lord right now; some of them even sits next to you in churches and yet the judgment of God is on their heads. Do not look at their faces, or their clothes or the way they sing, they are under the judgment of God.

How do you know if you are under the judgment of God? If you see that you cannot progress, you are troubled in your sleep, you are always moody, angry, depressed and sad and people cannot understand you. Those are the signs of someone under the torment of the tormentors. You are tormented and troubled because you have not released who God wants you to release and so the devil comes in with seven other evil spirits; pain, resentment, anger, bitterness, sadness and so on. And when God looks at you, he says to himself, I cannot bless you, I have given you already to the tormentors.

Jesus said that if you have unresolved issues, bitterness, anger growing up in your life and you are in a church, put your money on the offering table and go and reconcile and be delivered else, the strongman is going to destroy your life and your loved ones. If you have hatred in your life, you have got to deal with that strongman in your life. Ask for God's forgiveness and ask him to forgive you from the power of the strongman. You should also, forgive yourself. Forgive yourself from whatever mistake that you have made. Stop looking at yourself as defeated. God will forgive you of all what you have done so you can also forgive yourself. If you accept God's forgiveness for your life, you will move into greater things and the strongman will never be able to overpower you.

Chapter Reflections

1. _____
   _____

2. _____
   _____

3. _____
   _____

Chapter Sixteen

The Strong Man & The Spirits More Powerful Than Him

There is an enemy against your future and whether you believe it or not, there is an enemy that wants to destroy you. If you are involved in the things of God, the enemy is after you. This strong power that is against us is called the strongman. Many of the problems you are facing is not your fault. It is the fault of the strongman.

The minute you were born into this world, there was a strongman attached to your life and as you grew, you will recall that in different areas of your life you started finding struggles that you could not explain. It is the strongman operating; he is an invisible man operating behind the scenes. Consider whether there are demonic operation to destroy your life.

The strongman is not the devil. The devil has a kingdom in which these strongman work. Jesus has angels and he rules and reigns from above and we are a part of his Kingdom. Most times when persons preaches about the Kingdom of God, they say that He has riches and blessings and favor to give. Satan's Kingdom has the opposite of that to offer. That is why the Bible says in Colossians 1: 13 that he has delivered us from the power of darkness and hath translated us into the Kingdom of his dear son which is the Kingdom of Light.

So Jesus is the leader of the Kingdom of Light and his Kingdom has righteousness. Satan oversees the Kingdom of darkness, everything is wicked and evil where he also rules and reigns. There is an assignment of the strongman, for he is a worker of Satan.

The strongman does not like to be exposed. That is why, pastors and churches do not want you talking about demons, devils, and spiritual warfare, but those are a part of the ministry that Christ gave to the body of Christ. The strongman wants Christians to be in ignorance. He does not want them to know the truth. When you are ignorant of the strongman, he is happy.

The strongman has been on assignment and at every phase of your life, he intensifies his attack. There is a strongman assigned against your life, against your father, mother etc. There is a strongman attached to your family name. His assignment is not for you alone, after he is done, he comes for your family line and you therefore end up passing him to generations. Then he comes to destroy your whole clan, if he is not exposed and cast out. Some of you the strongman in the family is drunkenness and so everyone in that family is a drunkard.

How does the enemy operate? It is because there is a legal ground that the enemy is operating from. If you are in the things of God, the devil will do whatever it takes to take you away. So when he sees an open door, he sees it as an avenue to come into your life and operate. So be careful; some of the things that you are engaging yourself with is what the enemy might see as a legal ground for him to operate. You might not see it as wrong, but the enemy sees it as an avenue for him to come and attack you.

If you are not around people who are casting out demons, then you are powerless. Once you are not around a church casting out devils', then such church is powerless. The bible says that these are the signs that will follow them that believe; in his name they will cast out devils. These signs are meant to follow you everywhere you go. But today, I see Christians who cannot even cast out one little demon. If you can cast out devils, then you have got power.

The Pharisees knew about the casting out of demons but in this present age, we have Pastors and leaders who deny the power of the enemy. If Jesus cast out devils, then who are we? We are his disciples and so we are supposed to do the same thing.

If you were in your house, will you break up your furniture, break your possessions and break your things? No way! So also, any Kingdom brought against itself will be destroyed. The first thing you need to understand is that if you are going to go against the strongman then you cannot be divided. To destroy the enemy, you have to be unified. Well I know some of you have been praying and some of you have been binding, so before you start binding, come into unity. Because Satan's greatest tactic is to bring division.

Whatever we do, we try to keep our family united so that whenever we stand, there is Kingdom authority backing it up. Do not allow the devil to divide your house. Take a stand with your wife/husband and fight in the Holy Ghost. Be careful of the strongman because while you are asleep, he is already planning out his next attack.

Some of you were at the wrong place at the wrong time and so you made friends there and they messed your life up. You look back at that day and you say you wished you could reverse it. Sometimes when you were not prayerful and your spiritual life was going down the enemy was able to launch a successful attack. The Kingdom of God is the only thing that can cast out the devil. What is the Kingdom of God? It is also the power of God, the glory of God, the anointing of God. Demons cannot stand the power of the Kingdom of God.

Be careful of the strongman.

The devil is a counterfeit. He also wants to come and dwell in your life, and most people do not know this. Many people are filled with the strongman. As you go about from now on and you see people behaving a certain way, you will know that there is a strongman operating in their life. He controls them and makes them do things they do not even want to do— sometimes without realizing.

When the strongman is in a person, he does not want to leave his palace. But guess why the strongman does that? He was given the right to. He did not come in on his own, he had legal ground. He sees someone drinking once and he uses that opportunity to enter the person. He sees someone gambling and he uses that to enter the person. He sees someone watching pornography and uses that legal ground to come in. Unfortunately, the strongman does not stop a person from going to church; in fact, he allows him/her to go. That is why you see fornicators in church, you see adulterers in church, and you see drug dealers in church. He does not stop them from going to church; he does not care about church. And he uses that to deceive them to thinking that they are still good to go. He laughs and enjoy that person going to church because the church is powerless and he is not being called out. He loves religious people.

When the strongman has complete possession of the house; he controls the life of the person he is inside just like the way a house owner does in his own house. Since he is inside the house and he has no other job than to destroy, he begins to destroy everything in the house. He goes into the person's marriage and destroys it, he goes into the person's finances and destroys it, He goes into the person's health and destroys it and he goes into the person's dreams and destroys it. He just keeps destroying every aspect of the person's life. The strongman strategically works in every aspect of their life and destroys it.

One of the reasons why you should not have an area of weakness is because it gives the devil a space or a legal ground in your life. Do not give the devil a space or a legal ground. Jesus spent thirty years preparing for 3 years of ministry. Most people spend 3 years preparation for thirty years of ministry. Jesus is God in the flesh and he could have started his ministry at the age of twelve, he could have started his ministry at the age of fifteen, why did he have to wait till the age thirty? He waited for the preparation and the training and he faced temptations and faced the devil. When he overcame and became victorious, and the strongman came, he said to the strongman you can find nothing in me (John 14: 30). The priests emerges at age 30 in Jesus' culture.

You should always be binding the strongman; do not wait till he comes after you. Whenever you and the Holy

Spirit binds the strongman in your life, you get the spoils. What are the spoils? They are your inheritance, your blessings. You have so many miracles, many blessings and glory tied up but the strongman has restricted you.

What does the strongman do? He takes away your spoil, your blessings and stops your prayers from being answered. Daniel had been fasting and praying for about three weeks and yet even though God had sent the answer, the Prince of Persia delayed the angel brining the answer (Daniel 10:13).

The Lord has answered your prayers a long time ago but the strongman blocks them up. We should not be angry with God; it is not that he hasn't answered our prayers. That nasty devil and the strongman have blocked the answers to prayers. And that is why we are supposed to be binding the strongman; stripping him of all his powers in our life.

The first way to close the door of the strongman in your life is to confess your sin. When he sees that you are repenting of your sin, he begins to lose power. You are removing the legal ground of his existence. Take away the legal ground of the enemy while you confess. When you repent, it is another strong blow to his face. If you cannot repent, you have a strongman of pride. And it can destroy you more than anything else. If you have done anything wrong, admit it, we have all sinned and fallen short of God's glory (Romans 3:23).

From the first day you knelt down to pray, God heard you and wanted to answer you but there was a war in the heaven with the strongman. No wonder the bible says that we do not wrestle against mere humans but against principalities and powers etc. And these principalities stay and operate in the heavens. Your warfare is in the heavens. Stop casting and praying against your family and your friends but instead focus your prayers on the principalities and forces against your prayers. These strong spirits fought against the angel Michael and if Daniel had not continued to fast and prayed nothing will change (Daniel 10: 1 – 13).

Be careful of the strongman.

Now you may not see the strongman, but the bible is already saying that there is an unclean spirit. When the unclean spirit comes out of your life, he walks around dry places (Luke 11: 24). He is not happy as he is walking around; he wants to stay inside a person. He wants to be in human bodies because that is how he can execute the greatest destruction. Before Jesus came, no one was casting out demons but Jesus came and demonstrate the Kingdom of God. And so when you get delivered, do away with it completely. You have to see to it that you no longer have any relationship with whatever it is that you were delivered from.

I recalled one deliverance session where a confessed believer in Christ had begun to manifest in a service.

She had a wonderful voice to worship but could not get or hold a job and had apparent mental issues, especially delusions. That particular young lady was delivered from 25, 000 demons. Yes, I reiterate 25,000. Of course, it would have taken all night plus more to cast all of them out, but by the power and leading of the Holy Spirit we were able to identify the strong man that was working and bound all off them together and cast them out. Then there was another worker who worked as an Aid who got 15,000 demons cast out. Interestingly enough. On one occasion we encountered the spirit of a man's adulterous lover inside of her. The spirit in the woman began to talk like her husband's lover and declared her assignment was to kill the wife. If you are reading about this for the first time it is no joke. The spiritual world is very real.

I used to think that the strongman was wicked; but he has even seven spirits more wickedly than him. Therefore, if one does not walk in deliverance, confession their sins to the Lord for him to cleanse, the strong man will be back. If that newly delivered person does not feed up on the word of God to be washed (Isaiah 1:26, Ephesians 5:26), it will be back. And he makes them enter into that life and before you know it that man/woman is worse than he was before. No wonder you see great men of God who were burning for the Lord caught in a scandal of sleeping with women. Such a person becomes worse than he was before. He might have probably been involved with fornication and was later set free but when the enemy sees that he is now clean and empty; he uses that opportunity to invite seven other wicked spirits and makes him worse.

> *Repentance is the only way that you can be free from the strongman and this seven other spirits.*

Repentance is the only way that you can be free from the strongman and this seven other spirits. You have to repent today and ask God to save you from this strongman. Bind his powers and deliver yourself from the strongman and the seven other spirits.

Chapter Reflections

1. _____

2. _____

3. _____

Segment Four

Healing

Chapter Seventeen

Jesus The Healer

> *"Who his own self bare our sins in his own body on the tree, that we, being dead to sins, should live unto righteousness: by whose stripes ye were healed." – 1 Peter 2:24*

The world is sick, and it was because of this that Jesus came. Sicknesses or diseases were never part of God's agenda for humankind; it was the fall of man that exposed humanity to that demonic manipulation. No wonder, medical personnel will always ask questions from patients about their bloodline or family medical history.

The Bible said:

> "And Jesus went about all Galilee, teaching in their synagogues, preaching the gospel of the kingdom, and healing

> all kinds of sickness and all kinds of disease among the people. Then His fame went throughout all Syria; and they brought to Him all sick people who were afflicted with various diseases and torments, and those who were demon-possessed, epileptics, and paralytics; and He healed them. Great multitudes followed Him—from Galilee, and from Decapolis, Jerusalem, Judea, and beyond the Jordan."
> Matthew 4:23-25(NKJV),

In the scripture above, the Bible reveals the activity of Jesus in a region called Galilee, how He went about preaching the Gospel of the Kingdom. It is important to note that healing or miracle was not the first thing ascribed to Jesus in this scripture. Hence, in all His ministerial activities on earth, Jesus would always first preach the Gospel, for the salvation of the soul of men is much more important in the Kingdom. It is the foundation of any work of healing. Jesus' intention is to give the healing and miracle of the mind, body and spirit.

I have heard folks say that they have a healing ministry or miracle working ministry and nothing else, but then, how can that be true, when Jesus himself preached the Gospel of the Kingdom? It is important to first lay the foundation. Those healing, miracles, signs and wonders are not the end, the end is that men are saved into the Kingdom of God. Healing and miracles are the manifestations of the Kingdom of God.

> *Healing and miracles are the manifestations of the Kingdom of God.*

Now, a closer look at the scripture, Jesus healed all manner of sicknesses and diseases. A sickness is not the same as a disease. Just as its name implies, a disease is dis-ease, a form of discomfort. However, when the sickness affects a body organ, it becomes a disease. Such as High blood pressure (sickness) can lead to Heart Failure (disease) or Dementia (disease). High Cholesterol (sickness) causes Peripheral Arterial Disease. Sickness can be as little as just not feeling well. Cases can go away in the short term or develop into something worse such as a disease. One can feel ill (not well) because someone embarrass him/her or sick from having "butterflies in the stomach" because of anxiety. However, when that issue affects negatively the normal functionality of the body it is disease.

From the passage above, "**Then His fame went throughout all Syria; and they brought to Him all sick people who were afflicted with various diseases and torments, and those who were demon-possessed, epileptics, and paralytics; and He healed them.**" Notice that they brought to him sick people who were afflicted with various diseases and torments. When a person is discomforted, and one or more organ in his/her body already getting affected, the individual is definitely going through a great torment. Jesus healed those who were demon-possessed, epileptic and paralyzed. The Bible says; **"...and He healed them all"**.

It is high time you believed there is no sickness that Jesus cannot heal. None of those folks brought to Him went back home the same way they came; He healed them all. You really have to believe in the power of God to heal you. No matter what your own sickness or disease may be. Whether you are sick in your mind, or you are currently being tormented by disease in your body, all you need to do is to commit your spirit to Jesus. Just because the healing of your spirit is very important in preparing your mind and body for His touch. You really need to believe in the power of God, because when God moves in His power, He moves supernaturally.

The Causes of Sickness

Sicknesses and diseases can be traced to the following;

1. The Fall of Man
2. Sin
3. The Environment

As I cited earlier, the fall of man brought sicknesses and diseases as a curse on humanity. When the spirit of man got sick, it spreads into the mind and then the body. The evil deeds of men began to expose humanity to a whole lot of toxic things that are capable of damaging the human body. Sin increased on the surface of the

Jesus healed those who were demon-possessed. earth, and death became a constant experience, for the scripture says, "The wages of sin is death"(Romans 6:23). One may that die physically but a dream may die, a Godly opportunity may die, and a relationship or progress may die. One's will may die where he or she becomes consumed by drugs and alcohol.

Different kinds of human activities also made the atmosphere so polluted. The air became toxic repeatedly, and the environment is no longer safe like it used to be. Then, the good news is, those who believe in the power of God to save, also have access to the power of God to heal and deliver.

How to Receive From God

Let us take a quick look at the book of Matthew, chapters 8 and 9, as we analyze the events in these scriptures in relation to the power of God to heal and to perform miracles.

> "When He had come down from the mountain, great multitudes followed Him. And behold, a leper came and worshiped Him, saying, "Lord, if You are willing, You can make me clean." Then Jesus put out His hand and touched him, saying, "I am willing; be cleansed." Immediately his leprosy was cleansed. And Jesus said to him, "See that you tell no one; but go your way, show yourself to the priest, and offer

the gift that Moses commanded, as a testimony to them."
Matthew 8:1-4(NKJV)

In the Jewish custom, lepers are considered unclean, and so is anything they touch or anyone that touches them. However, right here, something significant happened. First, the leper worshipped Jesus as He was coming down from the mountain. Moreover, as he worshipped him, he said; "**Lord, if You are willing, You can make me clean.**"

Of course, Jesus saw more than his physical posture, He was able to see into his mind, and the leper's act of brokenness and sincerity moved Him that He did. Jesus was willing, and then, Jesus touched the leper. Jesus touched him.

Worship and Humility

If we know how to worship Him with all sense of sincerity there is nothing we cannot receive from God. Our acts of worship can reach out to Him, and make Him so obligated to attend to our needs. Jesus was supposed to become unclean touching the leper, but instead, His touch made the man clean. Glory! Only Jesus can touch an unclean thing and make it clean and yet remain clean.

Notice in the last verse that Jesus did not want him to publicize the healing, unlike what most ministers love doing in this present days. We want people to know that we have done a miracle. Mind you; we forget that it is not because we can, by our own natural instinct or ability, but simply because God has decided to empower us to be able to do so.

Several times in the ministry of Jesus Christ, two expressions are common in his healing events. The Bible would say "He healed them" or "He made them whole". Healing them is much more physical than making them whole. Making whole is a complete healing that affects every aspect of a human life. It is important to note that, it is not only that Jesus can heal you physically; He is also able to touch your life and make you whole. When He makes you whole, every aspect of your life is touched; your experience of healing will not only be physical but in all ramifications.

I have heard folks say that "God places sicknesses on people to humble them", that is not true. God does not need to place sickness on anyone to humble him or her. Sickness is not our teacher, and the Holy Spirit is. If anyone is sick, it is not because God wants them to be sick or remain sick, it is the intention of God that everyone sick is healed.

Faith Is Needed

> The Bible said, "Now when Jesus had entered Capernaum, a centurion came to Him, pleading with Him, saying, "Lord, my servant is lying at home paralyzed, dreadfully tormented."

> And Jesus said to him, "I will come and heal him." The centurion answered and said, "Lord, I am not worthy that You should come under my roof. But only speak a word, and my servant will be healed. For I also am a man under authority, having soldiers under me. And I say to this one, 'Go,' and he goes; and to another, 'Come,' and he comes; and to my servant, 'Do this,' and he does it." When Jesus heard it, He marveled, and said to those who followed, "Assuredly, I say to you, I have not found such great faith, not even in Israel!"
> In Matthew 8:5-10

The Centurion in the scripture above demonstrates a high level of faith in Jesus like nobody else. His servant was ill and he needed Jesus to heal his servant from paralysis. Jesus agreed, but this centurion spoke from a revelation perspective that made Jesus marvel. He acknowledged Jesus as a man of authority, and He believed that all that Jesus needed to do was to command from where He was and his servant would be healed. He explained that if he being a commander could command his own servants and make them do according to his word, Jesus would be able to do much more. He could command healing from where He was and nothing would be able to stand against it.

Without faith, no man can receive anything from God. If only you have faith, you would be able to get that which you need from the Lord. Can your faith ever marvel God?

Can God ever be moved to give unto you your request by the quality of your faith? Do you have faith? If yes, then, you are qualified to receive anything you ask from the Lord. The question is, "How do I have faith?"

> "So then faith comes by hearing, and hearing by the word of God." (Romans 10:17 NKJV)

Anytime you are able to hold unto in His Word, He is obligated to doing it for you! If there is ever anything done by the ancient prophets in the Old Testament, Jesus was able to do much more. If He did it during his earthly ministry, He can do it again for you now.

There Is Nothing Impossible With Jesus

> The Bible said, "Now when Jesus had come into Peter's house, He saw his wife's mother lying sick with a fever. So He touched her hand, and the fever left her. And she arose and served them." When evening had come, they brought to Him many who were demon-possessed. And He cast out the spirits with a word, and healed all who were sick, that it might be fulfilled which was spoken by Isaiah the prophet, saying: "He Himself took our infirmities and bore our sicknesses." Matthew 8:14-17(NKJV)

I hope you know that it is illegal for sickness to rule in your body, most especially, if you believe in the name of Jesus Christ.

Jesus went further in the same scripture and He demonstrated another dimension like never before. Matthew 8:23-27(NKJV);

> "Now when He got into a boat, His disciples followed Him. And suddenly a great tempest arose on the sea, so that the boat was covered with the waves. But He was asleep. Then His disciples came to Him and awoke Him, saying, "Lord, save us! We are perishing!" But He said to them, "Why are you fearful, O you of little faith?" Then He arose and rebuked the winds and the sea, and there was a great calm. So the men marveled, saying, "Who can this be, that even the winds and the sea obey Him?"

They were in the boat, and then there was a storm. The wind was blowing so seriously, but Jesus was asleep. The disciples thought they were going to die, it was that intense, but Jesus was still asleep; what manner of man is this that sleeps in the middle of a storm?

Understand this, if Jesus is in your ship, you cannot die, no matter how hard the wind may blow. To prove that Jesus has power over the natural realm, He spoke to the wind and right there before them all, the storm ceased. I do not know the kind of raging storm that is blowing so hard against you now? If only you can believe in Jesus Christ, you should be rest assured that in His name even the storms and the winds obey.

More Accounts of the Miracles of Jesus

In Matthew 8:28-34(NKJV), we are told about the deliverance of the man with the Legion. It said;

> "When He had come to the other side, to the country of the Gergesenes, there met Him two demon-possessed men, coming out of the tombs, exceedingly fierce, so that no one could pass that way. And suddenly they cried out, saying, "What have we to do with You, Jesus, You Son of God? Have You come here to torment us before the time?" Now a good way off from them there was a herd of many swine feeding. So the demons begged Him, saying, "If You cast us out, permit us to go away into the herd of swine. "And He said to them, "Go." So when they had come out, they went into the herd of swine. And suddenly the whole herd of swine ran violently down the steep place into the sea, and perished in the water. Then those who kept them fled; and they went away into the city and told everything, including what had happened to the demon-possessed men. And behold, the whole city came out to meet Jesus. And when they saw Him, they begged Him to depart from their region."

Notice vividly here that the demons asked Jesus, "Have You come here to torment us before the time?". It can be deduced from there that torment is not meant for humans but for demons. Hence, any experience of torment is a demonic manipulation. And just as they departed from the man as Jesus commanded them, you can command demons to lose their grip over your life in Jesus name!

Another account can be seen here in Matthew 9:1-8 (NKJV). It said;

> "So He got into a boat, crossed over, and came to His own city. Then behold, they brought to Him a paralytic lying on a bed. When Jesus saw their faith, He said to the paralytic, "Son, be of good cheer; your sins are forgiven you." And at once some of the scribes said within themselves, "This Man blasphemes!" But Jesus, knowing their thoughts, said, "Why do you think evil in your hearts? For which is easier, to say, 'Your sins are forgiven you,' or to say, 'Arise and walk'? But that you may know that the Son of Man has power on earth to forgive sins"—then He said to the paralytic, "Arise, take up your bed, and go to your house." And he arose and departed to his house. Now when the multitudes saw it, they marveled and glorified God, who had given such power to men."

Notice in verse two that the Bible says, "And when Jesus s*aw* their faith..." The question is, "How come their faith was visible that Jesus was able to see it? You cannot just claim to have faith in your heart; you must also show it in your acts. Faith is best known when it is shown.

> "While He spoke these things to them, behold, a ruler came and worshiped Him, saying, "My daughter has just died, but come and lay your hand on her and she will live." So Jesus arose and followed him, and so did His disciples. And suddenly, a woman who had a flow of blood for twelve years came from behind and touched the hem of His garment. For she said to herself, "If only I may touch His garment, I shall be made well." But Jesus turned around, and when He saw her He said, "Be of good cheer, daughter; your faith has made you well." And the woman was made well from that hour. When Jesus came into the ruler's house, and saw the flute players and the noisy crowd wailing, He said to them, "Make room, for the girl is not dead, but sleeping." And they ridiculed Him. But when the crowd was put outside, He went in and took her by the hand, and the girl arose. And the report of this went out into all that land." Matthew 9:18-26(NKJV),

A ruler came to ask Jesus to heal his sick daughter, and right there on the way, the miraculous happened. A woman with the issue of blood took a step of faith by believing that if only she could touch Jesus, she would be made whole. In spite of the crowd, Jesus

And when Jesus saw their faith...

was able to discern that touch of faith and distinguished it from a regular touch. Her display of faith justifies the fact that once there is a contact, the miraculous happens, irrespective of who is doing the touching. Jesus has always touched people, but then, this woman by her faith introduced a new dimension of possibility; "**if only I can touch the helm of His garment, I will be healed**".

Whatsoever you are believing God for, have the assurance that He is more than able to make it available. The Scripture says in Hebrews 12:2 (NKJV), "**Looking unto Jesus, the author and finisher of our faith, who for the joy that was set before Him endured the cross, despising the shame, and has sat down at the right hand of the throne of God.**"

Do not expect your healing or miracle to come from any man, believe in the power of Jesus to heal and do miracles. Look unto Him, and He shall deliver unto you that which you are asking Him for. Ask Him now, ask him with all sense of worship; He is right there by your side to deliver that which you're trusting Him for unto you.

Chapter Reflections

1. _____
   _____

2. _____
   _____

3. _____
   _____

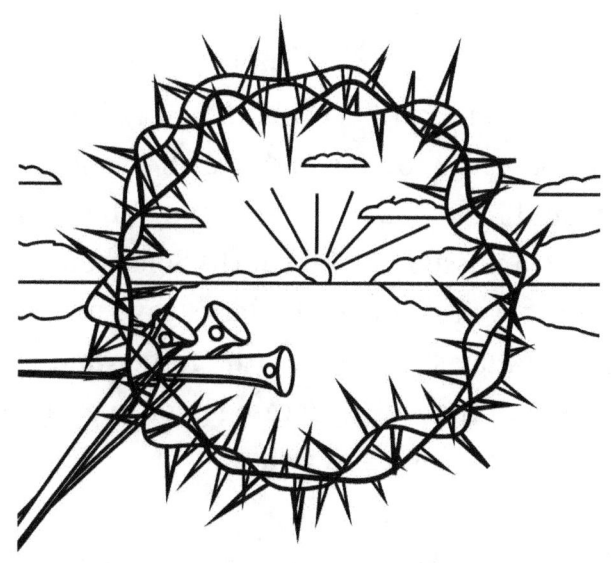

Chapter Eighteen

The Father Gives Zoë Life

> John 10:10 "The thief cometh not, but for to steal, and kill, and to destroy: I am come that they might have life, and that they might have it more abundantly."

*J*esus emphatically declares that one of His assigned purposes for coming to the earth was so that mankind would have this noble existence. The Father sent Jesus with a mission to die that His Sons would live.

Another writer states that Jesus gave up the abundance and majestic life with the father and with the agreement of the Father became poor to establish His Sons access to wealth and riches.

> "For ye know the grace of our Lord Jesus Christ, that, though He was rich, yet for your sakes He became poor, that ye through His poverty might be rich." Corinthians 8:9

What an amazing Father; He sacrificed His greatness of continuous worship and praises; crown of precious jewels and throne of authority to be born in a humble stable to establish our wealth.

This is similar in many ways to great earthly fathers who work long hard hours, giving us their own pleasures and even dreams to provide food and college fees so that their children can have a better life than they had.

The Father of Glory was willing to give His children resources so that they can excel in this life.

> Behold what manner of love the Father hath bestowed upon us that we should be called the Sons of God: therefore the world knoweth us not, because it knew Him not." I John 3:1

Zoë life from the Father

The Father is filled with love towards the lives of His children. In the dawn of the greatest period of mankind, an era of technological and medical breakthroughs papa wants to give the gift of the Holy Spirit and a superior life on earth. All across races, cultures, socio-economic and nations humans are in search of a people or grouping of people who exhibit peace in the midst of personal and international turmoil. Mankind is troubled with volatile financial and economic markets across the world. He is now in search of the truth in a creator. In fact, many reading this book are still in search of purpose in life.

Yet in the rubble of torn lives the loving Father says and yearns to give His children life and a peacefully purpose-motivated shalom life. Life that is satisfied from the internal peace in Christ and not from the external achievement of career, business, and wealth accumulation or even family or intimate relations.

His Zoë life is the power life that He gives to enablement to overcome struggles of depression, lust, sexual perversion, homosexuality, lesbianism, bestiality, fornication, lying, and deception. His Zoë life will melt away the lives of scars in His Sons.

It is the Father's good pleasure to give us:

- The keys to His Kingdom.
- The Kingdom implanted into the believer's life.
- Kingdom ruler-ship in the earth.

> Luke 12:31-32 "But rather seek ye the kingdom of God; and all these things shall be added unto you. (vs. 32) "Fear not, little flock; for it is your Father's good pleasure to give you the Kingdom."

> Luke 22:29 "And I appoint unto you a kingdom, as my Father hath appointed unto me..."

The physician Luke records the profound revelation of the search and fulfilment of every individual. The pursuit of life as stated by the master teacher and life coach; Jesus, is to seek after the knowledge of the Kingdom of God. Every individual is to look for the understanding and experience of the operation of the Heavenly Father's ruler ship both in heaven and in the earth. These transforming insights of man's identity can be fulfilled in the experience of the rule of Christ. Jesus prefaces these words with the meaning of man's existence. He warns of a life of anxiety and fear; and condemns an existence of only earth gratification.

Jesus warns that individuals should not be overwhelmed with solely the consumption of food, clothing and desires. He expresses that life is more valuable than the consumption of foods and the pursuits of clothing. Jesus condemns the destructive nature and habit of worrying about life. He defends the nature of the Father to provide for His children by comparing His provision for the birds. He articulates that the Father arrays the magnificent fields of flowers, lays down the grass hills and with His Word can cause them to wither away.

Jesus declares that mankind should not seek what they should eat or drink. His claim is that the children who are of the world; other nations consume their lives on these materials. Jesus is not denying the obvious needs and reality of food, clothes and shelter for persons.

However, the emphasis for effective existence should not hinge on these desires.

He emphatically express that the Heavenly Father knows that His Sons have needs while living in the Earth. The Heavenly Father has pre-knowledge of every general and specific need of His children. (Including general necessities, the provision of food) The Father created our bodies, and designed the organs to generate energy through food sources.

He realizes the energy for breathing, working and performing activities demand an energy source. He made the body with these mechanisms. He therefore is critically aware of the needs of the human body.

Jesus is reminding mankind that they are not petitioning the Father of an area He is not aware of. The request or passionate pursuit of food over the pursuit of the Father could be very insulting to the Lord. The product is telling the manufacturer what it needs to function, when he already knows.

Jesus speaks that the Father knows that His children has these needs. Hence, it can be presumed that the Father has made abundant provisions to supply every need. He has everything for our existence in the earth in store for His Sons. Hallelujah!

Luke 11:11 "If a son shall ask bread of any of you that is a Father, will he give him a stone? Or if he asks a fish, will he for a fish give him a serpent? (vs. 12) "Or if he shall ask an egg, will he offer him a scorpion? (vs. 13) "If ye then, being evil, know how to give your children good gifts, how much more shall your heavenly Father give the Holy Spirit to them that ask him?"

Jesus parallels a son asking an earthly father for food and receiving it. He states that an earthly father would not insult the child request and need for bread by giving a stone. The act of giving a stone demonstrates the lack of understanding of the child's requests, his needs and mocks his request. By not fulfilling the specific request of the child, the father could damage the relationship with His son; and cause mistrust of the son to the father. The father then insults the request of the son by giving him an object that is edible. The earthly father gives even animals that are potentially poisonous to His son. Jesus concludes that even the earthly father yearns to fulfil the request of the son to experience the joys of being a provider. The earthly father desires to observe the joys, excitement and gratification of the son with the provision of the earthly father.

Jesus states that earthly father knows how to give good gifts to their children. Therefore the Heavenly Father knows how to give the greatest gift to His Sons – the Holy Spirit. Within the package of the gift of the Holy Spirit resides the keys and direction to achieving everything material and spiritual need in the earth.

The Kingdom given by the Father:

> I Corinthians 15:24-28 "Then the end will come when He hands over the kingdom to God the Father after He has destroyed all dominion, authority and power."(vs. 25) "For He must reign until He has put all His enemies under His feet."(vs. 26) "The last enemy to be destroyed is death."

> I Corinthians 15: (vs. 27) "For He hath put all things under His feet. But when He saith, all things are put under Him it is manifest that He is excepted, which did put all things under Him. (vs. 28) "When He has done this, then the son Himself will be made subject to Him who put every-thing under Him, so that God may be all in all."

> Hebrews 2:9 "But we see Jesus, who was made a little lower than the angels for the suffering of death, crowned with glory and honour; that He by the grace of God should taste death for every man." (vs. 10) "For it became Him, for whom are all things, and by whom are all things, in bringing many sons unto glory, to make the captain of their salvation perfect through sufferings. (vs. 11) "For both He

that sanctifieth and they who are sanctified are all of one: for which cause He is not ashamed to call them brethren." (vs. 12) "Saying, I will declare thy name unto my brethren, in the midst of the church will I sing praise unto thee."

Ephesians 2:4 "But God who is rich in mercy for His great love where with He loved us" (vs. 5) "Even when we were dead in sins, hath quickened us together with Christ, (by grace ye are saved,). (vs. 6) "And hath raised us up together, and made us sit together in heavenly places in Christ Jesus: (vs. 7) "That is the ages to come He might show the exceeding riches of His grace in His kindness towards us through Christ Jesus."

Sketched deep in time was a broken family relationship between God and His prized possession, man. This distorted and disjointed body caused the world to be in a state of uproar and disorder. Mankind was no longer hearing the strong correction of the father nor His graceful encouragement. Instead, mankind was guided and governed by the rigidity of the laws of God and His appointed leaders. These selective leaders were teachers of the scripture, Judges, Kings, Prophets and Priests of the nation.

These officers were established to govern and rule the people of Israel into the purposes of God until such a time when the King Jesus would be their personal consultant, confident and friend.

Finally, in the silence of God's prophetic voice in the earth arose the promise, the repairers of the gap, the son Jesus Christ. *"In the fullness of times, God sent forth His Son, born of a virgin."*

The time had fully come; God desired to call His Sons back to Himself, and His voice would now be heard. His sons would now have direct access to His warm embrace, His gentle words of comfort and correction.

Jesus was now here on earth to pull the fellowship of heaven with the sons of the earth to accomplish the will of the father in the earth. Jesus is described as the first begotten son of the Father. He was the first lineage God was about to create. Jesus was the new model for many after who would long for a life that was obedient to the will and purpose of the Father in the earth. He was the first of this lineage to reveal the understanding of what is truly meant to walk with the Father and to continually have communion with Him. He proved to the world that the Father longs for a more intimate relationship with man that surpasses the formalities of religion and ethical living.

He proved that the Father still talks to His people even in a time of colossal organizational, technological and human advancement. Jesus proved that God still crave for man to understand their true identity in the midst of strong cultural and ideological times in which they lived. Most importantly, Jesus exhibited through His life the initial purpose that the Father wishes to execute His love, mission, order and will through His precious Sons in the earth. *"To those that are led by the spirit, to them He gave the power to become the Sons of God."*

The *Lexical Aids* to the New Testament states that the word 'Power' or 'Exousia (Greek) portrays the following meanings:

- Permission
- Authority
- Right
- Liberty

The word '**Exousia**' also denotes '**executive power**'. It emphasizes justified, having the right to exercise power. Right and might to exercise power. Similarly, to any nation on earth, various positions on the legal system or judiciary signify authority. For example, a judge or police has the power, to execute justice or make transaction on behalf of that nation. Hence, if individuals violate any of the laws prescribed by the country; the police can use the authority conferred upon them to make an arrest on behalf of the state.

This very same principle applies to the legal authorization conferred upon the believer by a loving Father to represent His name and enforce His agenda in the earth.

The believer has been given the full assurance that we can transact on behalf of Christ Jesus in the earth.

The disarray, disorder, abuse and destruction of millions of lives are simply a ripple effect of broken, misunderstood and absent identity in God the Father. The earth and mankind has lost seeing who they are. It reminds me of an illustration of peering into a looking glass. The more one looks into it the more the features of the face are observed. The blemish that was unnoticed a week prior can now be brilliantly observed. The colour of your eyes and skin completion is illuminated by looking into the mirror.

The more time spent in His presence the more we begin to see Him and understand Him. It is through this reflection that we begin to understand out true self. We begin to see areas that need it be developed and even seek for repentance and change. Maybe it is an attitude that needs correcting, a mind-set that continues to hinder us and fear about our own insufficiencies are minded in the presence of the Lord.

Our strengths are reaffirmed; our gifts are clearly outlined and enjoyed. The purposes of our lives are made clear and precise in the presence of the Lord.

In the presence of the Lord, we are constantly made and formed into the very image of Christ. The word of God says *"We are as looking glass,"* we reflect His image and glory. Jesus came in the likeness, fullness and glory of the Father. He was the expressed image of the Father according to the book of Hebrews. He was in the splendour of the Father because of His continuous fellowship.

Jesus lived to fulfil a number of responsibilities including salvation, restoration and the shedding of His precious blood for the remission of sin.

However, there was another unspoken mission that has been overlooked through the centuries; Jesus came to restore the broken identity of man. He came to raise many sons in the exact same image of His life and to adopt those who were by nature outside of the family and covenant of God. According to Old Testament scripture only those who were direct lineage and offspring of Abraham and Israel had rights to have fellowship and blessings with God. However, God wanted to be an active father to all of humanity. He had to re-establish the true identity of humanity.

This identity is not from graduating from a prestigious university, neither descendants of a wealthy family, nor possession of talents and gifting. A true nature of a person is whom you were created to be and fulfilled in Jesus.

> I John 5:7-8 "For there are three that bear record in heaven the Father, the Word and the Holy Ghost; these three are one." (vs. 8) "And these are three that bear witness in earth,

the spirit and the water. And the blood and these three agree in one."

Another account **John 1:1-4; 14** *"In the beginning was the word, and the word was with God and the Word was God.*

(vs. 2) "The same was in the beginning with God." (vs. 3) "All things were made by Him; and without Him was not anything made that was made. (vs. 4) "In Him was life, and the life was the light of men." (vs. 14) "And the word was made flesh and dwelt among us, (and we beheld His glory, the glory as of the only begotten of the Father, full of grace and truth."

The beloved Apostle John wrote of the mystery of the (trichotomy) three in one God. This wonder will forever remain glorious that the Father, Jesus the Son and the Holy Spirit are one in nature, character, purpose and agreement. The above scripture outlines that in the Heavens that the Father, <u>the Word</u> and the Holy Spirit are one.

The *Lexical Aids* to the New Testament states that the definition of The Word (3056) is logos. **Logos** comes from the root word 'Lego' to speak by linking and knitting together connected discourse the inward thoughts and feelings of mind.

Logos expresses thought, intelligence and also which expresses it **"Logos** when it refers to discourse, it is regarded as the orderly linking and connecting together in corrected arrangement of words of the inward thoughts and feeling of the mind.

Hence Jesus is expressed as the word which is the personal manifestation, most only a part of the divine nature of the Father, but expresses thought, nature and totality of all the ideas and words of the Father.

> John 1:1-18 "No man hath seen God at any time; the only begotten Son, which is in the bosom of the Father, He hath declared Him."

These scriptures further clarify Jesus as the totality of the nature, thoughts, word and expressed image of the Father. This is especially so that mankind may briefly grasp the glory of the Father Jehovah. The writer states that from the beginning the 'Word' was and existed with the Father and the 'Word' was God.

It elaborates that the 'Word' was in the beginning with God and everything was made by the word. The 'Word' was the architect of all that existed in the universe. In the Word, the Zoë life, the life that is complete, abundant and of the highest order when man accepts the word.

The writer then expresses in **John 1:14.** *"And the word was made flesh..."* the God of the universe who sat in the heavens ruling with royalty, sovereignty and power receiving glory due to Him came to earth. The word who formed the superstructure of the universe in the power of Hs glory; who spoke all that exist with His word of power stepped into an earthen body.

The Word who in **Genesis 1:28** decided to form the clay container of man to host the spirit of man himself, stood in the temporal dirt suit.

The word dwelt among humans in their form but expressed fully the nature and thoughts of God the Father.

The writer John states that *"men saw His glory and the glory was the glory of the only begotten of the Father."* As we recall the term **glory**, is not a mystical, deep and spooky concept. The word '**Glory**' means the nature character, majesty, weight of wealth, splendor, riches and royalty. Hence Jesus the word portrays the splendor of the Father's lifestyle and wealth. Hallelujah!!!

The term only begotten (3439), '**Mono-genes**' means **mono**-only and **gene** to form, to make. "**Monogenes**" means the only one of the family. Only John uses **Monogenes** to describe the relationship of Jesus to God the Father, presenting Him as the unique one, the only one (monos) of the family genos in the discussion of the relationship of the son to the father."

The 'genos' from which the word genes in 'monogenes' originally means stock, race and family.

The expression 'monogenes' as in genos Jesus Christ designated as the only one of the same stock in the relationship of the son to the Father. He is not to be understood as eternally born of the Father, but only in His humanity was He born. Therefore, mono genes can be held as synonymous with the God-man. We gather the concept of the word is Jesus and Jesus is the only one of the kind that came from the Father. He is God in the flesh.

The prophetic writer Isaiah peered through times and down age to glimpse the glory of the Father in the person of Jesus Christ. He captured the fullness of Jesus, His nature, His assignment, purpose and eternal plan to establish His Kingdom.

> Isaiah 9:6-7 "For unto us a Child is born, unto us a son is given and the government shall be upon His shoulder and His name shall be called wonderful Counsellor, The mighty God, The everlasting <u>Father</u>, The Prince of Peace. (vs. 7) "Of the increase of His government and peace there shall be no end, upon the throne of David, and upon His Kingdom, to order it and to establish it with judgment and with justice from henceforth even forever. The zeal of the Lord of will perform this."

Jesus the Word is described prophetically by Isaiah as the above titles only given to God the Father. He describes Jesus as the Wonderful and the mighty God! Praise God. This prophetic writer describes that this child born would be called by the name ascribe only to the Heavenly Father that is "the everlasting Father."

> Isaiah 7:14 "Therefore the Lord Himself shall give you a sign; behold, a virgin shall conceive, and bear a son, and shall call His name Immanuel."

> Matthew 1:18 "Now the birth of Jesus Christ was on this wise: where as His mother Mary was espoused to Joseph, before they came together, she was found with child of the Holy Ghost." (vs. 20) "But while he thought on these things behold, the angel of the Lord appeared unto him in a dream, saying Joseph, thou son of David, fear not to take unto thee Mary thy wife for that which is conceived in her is of the Holy Spirit."(vs. 21) "And she shall bring forth a son, and thou shalt call His name JESUS: for He shall serve His people from their sins."

> Matthew 1: (vs. 23) "Behold a virgin shall be with child, and shall bring forth a son, and they shall call his name Emmanuel, which being interpreted is God with us."(vs.25)

> "And knew her not till she had brought forth her firstborn son: and he called His name Jesus."

The Apostle Matthew began his writing with the genealogy of Mary and Joseph the parental covering for Jesus. Joseph however, was not the natural father of Jesus but acted as a spiritual Father for Jesus. Joseph receives a confirmation for his uncertain heart concerning the emasculate conception of Jesus. An angel declared that Jesus was the result of the Holy Spirits conception and creative powers. The angels also expressed instructionally that the son's name should be called Jesus.

He is God in the flesh.

The definition of the name of **Jesus** is powerful to the nature, purpose and power of Sonship in Jehovah.

Jesus Christ is significant to the purpose of the Father to establish His Kingdom in the earth through the Sons. Jesus' life, words, authority and purpose represents that He is the authentic son of God. Jesus is referred to in scripture from the original text as '**Huios**', from the Greek means **"The Son."** He was not just any creation of God.

He is the actual person, very essence and expressed thoughts of the Father within the confines of human finite understanding.

Jesus' life is very significant to the present believer as He lived not just to establish the law and the new covenant but also to "...call many Sons." He came to establish as new lineage of believers who fellowship with God in a relationship. Adam was stated as the first man and Jesus is known as the second Adam. Like Adam, Jesus had no earthly Father. He was directly fathered only by the spirit of God.

Scientifically, the Father determines the blood production and type of its offspring. Hence, both Adam in the pre-fallen state and Jesus were sons with a pure line or genetic make-up. They were not formed in contamination or genes of a sinful nature. Adam was born sinless but was lead by the spirit-led life and not from the desires of fleshly appetites.

Adam fell to rebellion and disobedience in the Garden of Eden and not only died a spiritual death but later a physical death. Adam by deception gave his Kingdom dominion and sovereign rule, given by the Father's command to have dominion, over to earth to Satan.

> Genesis 2:16 "And the Lord God commanded the man saying of every tree of the garden thou mayest freely eat:" (vs. 17) "But of the tree of knowledge of good and evil, thou shalt not eat of it: for in the day that thou eatest there of thou shalt die."

The above scriptures outline the instruction of the Lord to Adam, the Father of all humans throughout the ages. Adam was commanded not to eat the fruit and the consequences were explained by the Father.

> Genesis 3:6 "And when the woman saw that tree was good for food, and that it was pleasant to the eyes, and a tree to be desired to make one wise, she took of the fruit thereof, and did eat, and gave also unto her husband with her; and he did eat."

The verse outlines the deception of the serpent to the mother of all humans Eve. She was beguiled by the lies of the serpent. She noted the fruit to be luring to her eyes. Eve gave Adam the fruit and He eats. He activated the process and penalty of sin in their lives. They both started the deterioration of death and the relinquishing of dominion authority to Satan.

Jesus therefore is vital to the restoration, redemption, re-establishment of the Sons of God to relationship with the Father. He came to establish a new lineage of Sons, those who will walk with the Father like Adam in His pre- fallen state.

Jesus from *Vine's Complete Expository Dictionary* of Old and New Testament word defined as the **Greek Ieseus** (2424) which is a translation of the Hebrew

"Joshua" meaning **"Jehovah is Salvation"** and **"the Saviour."** It was given to the son of God incarnation as His personal name, in obedience to the command of an angel to Joseph. The name Jesus has a prophetic declaration of His assignment from His glorious name.

Jesus was called by God to restore or place man back into His position of righteous government and authority under the sovereign partnership with Jehovah God.

The Father yearns for the restoration of His Sons. This word 'Son' from the original language and text has two words. One word definition is '**Tekna**,' which connotes a young child in reference to scripture; it suggests that all of humanity is the offspring or creation of God. However, the second term of **Huios** refers to a mature son.

The word 'son' is not a term of gender but one of relationship. It indicates position of fellowship and of God. These qualities lead to the maturity of a believer to that of a saint who has access and authority to conduct the will of God in the earth. This position of sonship crosses all manmade boundaries. It supervenes the ethnic, racial and socioeconomic limitations that have marginalize the believers from walking in their God given authority.

Sonship has unlimited potential to propel a believer unto every promise and blessing that the heavenly Father has in store through Jesus Christ.

Jesus, the firstborn son became the one through whom came many sons to the Father. Through Jesus the lost

Sons will learn the inheritance God has left. The world is introduced to the Royal family that the humanity can be adopted into the kingly family. We are children of the King.

Through intimately and intricately studying the life and ministry of Jesus the Holy Spirit will begin to gently whisper the mysteries of Jesus Christ. The life of those who seek restored fellowship with the Father will be opened to the process of daily development that God desires. Jesus makes many profound and bold claims that He and the Heavenly Father were one being.

> John 17:11 "And now I am no more in the world, but these are in the world and I come to thee. Holy Father, keep through thine own name those whom thou hast given me that they may be one as we are."

> John 17:21 "That they all may be one, as thou, Father, art in me, and I in thee, that they also may be one in us: that the world may believe that thou hast sent me."(vs. 22) "And the glory which thou gavest me I have given them; that they may be one, even as we are one:"

> John 17:(vs. 23) "I in them, and thou in me, that they may be made perfect in one; and that the world may know that thou hast sent me, and hast loved them, as thou hast loved

me." (vs. 24) "Father I will that they also whom thou hast given me He with me where I am; that they may behold my glory, which thou hast given me for thou lovedst me before the foundation of the world."

Our Lord Jesus in His intercessory prayer of **John 17** admonishes the Heavenly Father to restore Him to His former place of authority and majesty. He wanted to reclaim His place in the Heavenlies as supreme Lord and shed the earthen vessel. His assignment of relationship, restoration and re-establishing the Kingdom of the Father back to the executives in the earth was complete. Jesus had made all provisions and was embarking in the proceeding chapters to be the sacrificial lamb that would be slain so that man would be reconnected to the Father through Jesus' blood. Many who would believe would be given the power to become matured sons of God.

Jesus in a narrative manner communes with the Father, interceded for the Sons of God who walked with Him but also those who would be adopted into the Family of God throughout the ages. Jesus also reveals the mystery of our God; His ones with the Father. He states *"...that they may be one as we are one."* **John 17:11**

John 17 (vs. 21) "That they all may be one as thou, Father, art in me; and I in thee that they also may be one in us: that the world may believe that thou hast sent me."(vs. 22) "... that they may be one, even as we are one."

Other emphatic claims of His lordship are in **John 10:30** *"I and my Father are one." And in* **John**

> 10:38 "But if I do through ye believe not me, believe the works: that ye may know, and believe; that the Father is in me, and I in Him."

Praise God! Jesus is Lord of everything. Paul the Apostle in His writing to the believers and followers of Christ in Phillip reiterates the true identity of Jesus. Paul also powerfully utters the purpose and authority of Jesus over death, sin and every other name.

> Philippians 2:5 "Let this mind be in you, which was in also in Christ Jesus. (vs. 6) "Who being in the form of God, thought it not robbery to be equal with God: (vs. 7) "But made Himself of no reputation and took upon Him the form of a servant, and was made in the likeness of men:

> Philippians (vs. 8) "And being found in fashion as a man He humbled Himself, and became obedient unto death, even the death of the cross." (vs. 9) Wherefore God also hath highly exalted Him, and given Him a name which is above

every other name:(vs. 10) "That at the name of Jesus every knee should bow, of things in heaven, and things in earth and things under the earth;(vs. 11) "And that every tongue should confess that Jesus Christ is Lord, to the glory of God the Father."

This passage lays the foundation of Jesus being the nature and essence of the Heavenly Father. It articulates magnificently the process in which the Father wrapped Himself unassumingly in the suit of a baby in Mary's womb. He was driven by the passion into cross of death. His name is now highly exalted and glorified above every name of demons, diseases, conditions, circumstances and every enemy of the King's rule in our lives.

Halleluiah! His name also has authority in the heaven invisible and spheres throughout the universe.

Chapter Principles

- Jesus came to give an abundant life or nobler, highest form of human existence.
- Jesus left the majesty of heaven's royalty to become poor to give sons His royal nature and access.
- The Father appointed or conferred kingdom authority to His Sons.
- Jesus express that man's desire should be for the Kingdom and not for material possession.

- The Father knows the needs of His children but wants them to seek diligently their lost dominion in the Kingdom.
- The Kingdom authority has been delegated to faithful sons in the earth.
- The Spirit gives mankind the potential through obedience to become Sons of God.
- Jesus is the word of God the father.
- Jesus is the Father warmed in humanly form for the purpose of restoring mankind and being an eternal intercessor.
- Jesus is the Son of God; the only begotten of the Heavenly Father.
- Jesus is vital to the restoration, redemption, re-establishment of the Sons of God to relationship with the Father.

Chapter Reflections

1. _____

2. _____

3. _____

Chapter Nineteen

Health, Healing And Supernatural Healing

> *"Behold, I will bring it health and cure, and I will cure them, and will reveal unto them the abundance of peace and truth."*
>
> *– Jeremiah 33:6*

*T*he world is in crisis because of the current pandemic, and Jesus Christ is the only healer. The demand of God is that we heal the sick. Sickness came after the fall of man. Diseases and sicknesses are products of sin. The Bible says, "But He was wounded for our transgressions, he was bruised for our iniquities; the chastisement for our peace was upon Him, and by His stripes we are healed." (Isaiah 53:5 NKJV)

Jesus was wounded for our sins, and bruised for our iniquities. Jesus received 39 stripes not because it was easy, but because our healing is attached to the stripes. There is 39 classifications of Diseases. Jesus has paid the price for every aspect of human disease category. He paid it all. By His stripes, you are healed. You are not about to be healed, you are healed. He is not hoping to heal you; He has healed you already. Why do you still want to carry the infirmity that has been paid for?

Believers Have God's Healing Power Within

> The Bible says, "And these signs will follow those who believe: In My name they will cast out demons; they will speak with new tongues; they will take up serpents; and if they drink anything deadly, it will by no means hurt them; they will lay hands on the sick, and they will recover." (Mark 16:17-18 NKJV)

As a faith-believing Christian, you have the healing power of God in you. There are certain signs that will follow those who believe. We are not to follow these signs, but to follow the belief systems of God so that these signs can follow us.

In Luke 4:18-19, Jesus Christ said:

> "The Spirit of the Lord is upon Me, Because He has anointed Me to preach the gospel to the poor; He has sent Me to heal

the brokenhearted, to proclaim liberty to the captives and recovery of sight to the blind, to set at liberty those who are oppressed; to proclaim the acceptable year of the Lord."

Jesus Christ has many assignments, and these include to preach the Gospel to the poor, heal the brokenhearted, proclaim the liberty to the captives, set the oppressed at liberty and to proclaim the acceptable year of the Lord.

> "Whatever city you enter, and they receive you, eat such things as are set before you. And heal the sick there, and say to them, 'The kingdom of God has come near to you.'" (Luke 10:8-9 NKJV)

Your assignment is to preach the Gospel, and to heal the sick. Healing makes preaching easier. When people experience true healing, they become open to the Gospel of the Kingdom. The Bible says:

> "These twelve Jesus sent out and commanded them, saying: "Do not go into the way of the Gentiles, and do not enter a city of the Samaritans. But go rather to the lost sheep of the house of Israel. And as you go, preach, saying, 'The kingdom of heaven is at hand.' Heal the sick, cleanse the lepers, and raise the dead, cast out demons. Freely you have received, freely give." (Matthew 10:5-8 NKJV)

When Jesus sent the disciples, He gave them specific instructions. The priority is that they preach as they go, restore the lost, and heal the sick. The power of God follows His instructions. He instructed to preach, and alongside heal the sick, cleanse the lepers, raise the dead and cast our demons. This power was given freely, and we are to dissipate this power according to the will of God freely.

> "Bless the Lord, O my soul; and all that is within me, bless His holy name! Bless the Lord, O my soul, and forget not all His benefits: who forgives all your iniquities, who heals all your diseases, who redeems your life from destruction, who crowns you with lovingkindness and tender mercies, who satisfies your mouth with good things, so that your youth is renewed like the eagles." (Psalms 103:1-3 NKJV)

Praise be to God for the forgiveness of our iniquities, granted us healings from diseases and redemption from destruction of any form. Our healing is secured in God's redemption. We have an inheritance in Christ, and His redemption has paid for all of our sins, diseases and destruction. He renews our strength and youthfulness like the eagles.

Through faith, God, who cleanses us from all of our sins when we confess them, instantly and repeatedly heals us. The same faith I have in Jesus for forgiveness is also potent for my healing. He cleanses us, heals us and empowers us to heal others. What a mighty God!

Healing Through the Word of God

> "He sent His word and healed them, and delivered them from their destructions." (Psalms 107:20 NKJV)

The word of God is the prescription to every sickness, illness and destructions. When God wants to heal, He sends His word. His word carries power to heal, deliver and empower. The word of God can correct every malfunction in man. Keep confessing God's word over your life. The Holy Spirit is not left out in your healthy living; He gives the instructions you need for breakthrough. Just one word from God's word is enough to transform and heal your life.

> "The Lord builds up Jerusalem; He gathers together the outcasts of Israel. He heals the brokenhearted and binds up their wounds." (Psalms 147:2-3 NKJV)

God is building up His Jerusalem, and to achieve this, He gathers the lost, the outcasts and even those who are strangers to the commonwealth of Israel. He desires to raise an army of people who have sound minds and health. So He heals the brokenhearted, binds up the wounded and delivers the oppressed.

> "He is despised and rejected by men, a Man of sorrows and acquainted with grief. And we hid, as it were, our faces from Him; He was despised, and we did not esteem Him. Surely He has borne our griefs and carried our sorrows; yet we esteemed Him stricken, smitten by God, and afflicted. But He was wounded for our transgressions, He was bruised for our iniquities; the chastisement for our peace was upon Him, and by His stripes we are healed." (Isaiah 53:3-5 NKJV)

He Is Jehovah Rapha

In Hebrews, Health means 'Shalom'. Jesus' type of healing is Shalom, and this means completeness, wholistic. His healing is complete and total. Shalom type of health is not just getting healed or delivered from disease, but also getting healed from wrong mindsets, negative emotions, wrong mental construct, marital issues, etc.

Health also means 'Ralpha', meaning to restore, favor, cure, repair or make whole. It also means medicine. Healing is for the earth. It is only needed as long as we are on the surface of the earth. The healing power of God is not needed in heaven. Heaven is under the Sovereignty of God; however, the Devil and his agents is on the earth, going about to afflict the people of God with diseases. This is why God makes healing available for us on the earth. So that we can serve God in good health, and serve the purposes of God. We cannot preach the Gospel with sick bodies.

God can heal your body, soul and spirit. His power is not only limited to bodily ailments, but also to things that pertain to your heart, mind and soul. He can heal you of hurts, pain, trauma, heartbreak and mental problems.

The Bible says,

> "Why are you cast down, O my soul? And why are you disquieted within me? Hope in God; for I shall yet praise Him, the help of my countenance and my God." (Psalms 42:11 NKJV)

When your soul is cast down or depressed due to things happening around or in you, you can hope in God to quicken you. God is the help of your countenance. He can heal your countenance. Worshipping and blessing the name of the Lord attracts the healing power of God.

God is concerned about every aspect of your life. When Christ died for our salvation, He died to heal, deliver and set free. Your salvation package comes with healing, deliverance and liberty from the tyranny of flesh, worldliness and Satan. Salvation means to be healed, delivered and set free. Salvation is not complete without your sound mind and sound body.

Scriptures to Meditate On

- **"My son, do not forget my law, but let your heart keep my commands; for length of days and long life and peace they will add to you. Let not mercy and truth forsake you; bind them around your neck, write them on the tablet of your heart, and so find favor and high esteem in the sight of God and man. Trust in the Lord with all your heart, and lean not on your own understanding; in all your ways acknowledge Him, and He shall direct your paths. Do not be wise in your own eyes; fear the Lord and depart from evil. It will be health to your flesh, and strength to your bones. Honor the Lord with your possessions, and with the first fruits of all your increase; so your barns will be filled with plenty, and your vats will overflow with new wine."** (Proverbs 3:1-10 NKJV)

Jesus heals the unsaved too but for a purpose which is to make them come to the redeeming grace of God. If you are proud and arrogant, you will not be healed. If you do not honor and fear the Lord, you will not be healed. Your giving can cause currents of health to flow in your body also.

- "There is one who speaks like the piercings of a sword, but the tongue of the wise promotes health." (Proverbs 12:18 NKJV)
- "A wicked messenger falls into trouble, but a faithful ambassador brings health." (Proverbs 13:17 NKJV)
- "Pleasant words are like a honeycomb, Sweetness to the soul and health to the bones." (Proverbs 16:24 NKJV)
- "*Is* this not the fast that I have chosen: To loose the bonds of wickedness, to undo the heavy burdens, to let the oppressed go free, and that you break every yoke? *Is it* not to share your bread with the hungry, and that you bring to your house the poor who are cast out; when you see the naked, that you cover him, and not hide yourself from your own flesh? Then your light shall break forth like the morning, Your healing shall spring forth speedily, And your righteousness shall go before you; The glory of the Lord shall be your rear guard (Isaiah 58:6-8 NKJV)

You will never be healed speaking health and destruction. When you speak the word, you create an atmosphere for the healing power of God to flow in your environment. You do not have to be an Apostle, Prophet, Pastor, Teacher or an Evangelist to heal, all you need is to believe the word of God.

Chapter Reflections

1. _____
_____

2. _____
_____

3. _____
_____

Chapter Twenty

Ministering To The Sick

> *"Is any sick among you? Let him call for the elders of the church; and let them pray over him, anointing him with oil in the name of the Lord:" – James 5:14*

In Genesis chapter 1 and 2 in the creation story, we see that everything begins with God (Elohim) the Creator. We also see the fall of man. During the fall of man God cursed Adam and Eve in essence when He told them from dusts you are and from dusts you shall return, this is the beginning of the activation of death. Before then there was no such thing as death for man. After the fall of man God instituted the process of death. We begin to see the process of death into the lives of humans and through diseases etc. Death was initiated by rebellion; A rebellion which is sin. We know it says in Romans that the wages of sin is death, through one man Adam... (Romans 5:12).

Why is the ministering of health so important?

God began to make these promises as Moses brought them out of Egypt in Exodus Chapter 15:26.

It said:

> "And said, If thou wilt diligently hearken to the voice of the LORD thy God, and wilt do that which is right in his sight, and wilt give ear to his commandments, and keep all his statutes, I will put none of these diseases upon thee, which I have brought upon the Egyptians: for I am the LORD that healeth thee." (Exodus Chapter 15:26)

God initiated a simple guideline in the bible to be obedient to his laws. Because sin initiated death God had to bring about a mechanism whereby he could still keep His children and humanity healed. What an awesome God we serve. In spite of man's fall, God through His love (because God is love), initiated a system if two things.

1. To stay healthy and stay in the realm of healing

2. To provide a certain mechanism where God came down by angels, by prophets, by His holy people to heal His people.

In the New Testament we see the initiation and activation of the church and the eldership praying for the sick and the needy.

In Isaiah also, Jesus is fulfilling those his prophetic promises. Jesus came and the Bible said when the Messiah shall come He shall come with healing in His wings. That is not some wings that an angel or a chicken has. This is talking about tallit, that prayer shoal that they wore at that time. Jesus being a Rabi and of the origin of Jews of Judea, a Hebrew had the prayer shoal. With this prayer shoal the woman with the issue of blood touch the hem (of the tallit) which is called wings and she got supernatural healing.

God said if you obey my commandments as it says in Leviticus, then you will see how to live. Leviticus gives us an outline of food that we should not eat. Certain foods, certain animals carry certain bacteria and parasites; those infectious things that God wanted the children of Israel to stay away from. You are not going to hell if you eat swine and pork. However, there are some health benefits and risk from eating certain things, so one should obey God. Animals that are found on the road dead and decompose should not be eaten.

Be Holy as God is Holy. God wants His people to be Holy and set apart. Leviticus tells us of the law of eating and the law of food. Most of these diseases that we are seeing are not transmitted from person to person are rising; Diseases such as diabetes, hypertension, cardiovascular diseases, and heart attacks. The leading cause of amputation of the feet is diabetic, or dietetic complications that are not being controlled properly by patients.

These diseases are preventable if there is proper diet such as low salt diet, more fruits and vegetables. Even pressure can controlled by regulating sugar and cholesterol intake. Just make dieting changes. Not only is God love but He has placed health laws for the saints.

The Bible also talk about the male child, for example. On the 8th day the flesh of his foreskin shall be circumcised. Circumcision was Gods idea. Medical science knows today that if you circumcise a child that there are numerous health benefits.

God is a God concerned about our health. For example one can take more than 4 hours to prepare a turkey. If one take the time to do that and a pet comes and eats it, how would you feel about that? Or if you created an art work and someone comes and knocks it over, how would you feel? Likewise God loves His creation, our bodies are the temple of the Holy Spirit. How would you like to see your image smeared and destroyed or run down? God is interested in our health. Notice I did not say healing as yet. God is interested in health. In the book of Leviticus, God initiated the priest to be the medical practitioners. What a loving God we serve. The word priest means one who represents God to the people and the people to God.

The priest is the advocate and intercessor, Jesus is our high priest.

The priests were not only responsible for the religious and spiritual teaching of the laws and principle practices, but also the medical. God appointed the priests, the holy men of God to examine the people. If they had leprosy they were isolated, until they were cured, to prevent spreading. Their clothes, bedding, everything they sat on was to be taken and buried and destroyed. This was done as to not cause an outbreak in the nation of Israel.

Leviticus talks about the cleansing of the house and destruction of the house where there was leprosy. Largely, God wanted a clean whole healthy nation. This book also illustrated that if a man or woman has a discharge, him, her and anyone who touched them was to be separated (Leviticus 15). Note that, from medical science, the life is in the blood and that diseases are in every bodily fluid. The lymphatic, vaginal, anal, seaman, breast milk, saliva, spinal fluid can all be infectious.

Leviticus chapter 17:10 discusses another health issue dealing with the issue of blood. In our culture we are dealing with a lot of medium rare cooked food. In the Satanic or occult organization one of their main things is the drinking of either animal or human blood. That is a sign of a disobedient or rebellious nature, towards God's desire. God desires that none should drink or uses any blood for demonic purposes.

> "…..The blood is the life of all flesh…. (Leviticus 17:14)

We are not to eat raw or medium rare foods. It is of a satanic nature.

All of Leviticus and Numbers are dealing with the Hebrews as they are in the wilderness where the Lord instructed then on how to live holy and righteous. In the book of Deuteronomy which also talks about health, look at the blessing that comes with obedience and disobedience, especially in Deuteronomy 28:1-68.

"Now it shall come to pass, if you diligently obey the voice of the Lord your God, to observe carefully all His commandments which I command you today, that the Lord your God will set you high above all nations of the earth. And all these blessings shall come upon you and overtake you, because you obey the voice of the Lord your God ….." (Deuteronomy 28:1-2)

> "But it shall come to pass, if you do not obey the voice of the Lord your God, to observe carefully all His commandments and His statutes which I command you today, that all these curses will come upon you and overtake you…… (Deuteronomy 28:15)

God allows diseases to come upon those who disobey Him. For example f you obey God you will be healthy if you don't you will be sick. Thank God Isaiah talks about God who sent His word to heal our diseases, once reconciliation has taken place.

Elijah performed many miracles. Jesus himself was wounded for our transgressions and bruised for our iniquity. By His stripes we are healed. We are made whole, we are blessed. In the book of Matthew Jesus is setting up the model for the church to administer healing, in particular to those who believe. Jesus went about in Galilee teaching and preaching in the synagogues, the Gospel of the Kingdom and healing all manner of disease among the people. First Jesus preached the Gospel of the Kingdom, then He laid hands on the sick. He is triumphant sitting in the heavens making intercessory on behalf of the church. He has a Kingdom that has established in the earth. When you are born again you begin to possess of the Kingdom. In that, know that His Kingdom reigns. We are to pray for His Kingdom and represent His Kingdom. We are to do His works in the earth; spreading this Gospel of the Kingdom around the world. So that His name and power to rule in the earth.

The laws of God is the only thing that governs our lives. We are to seek first the Kingdom of God and His righteousness and everything we want in this life will be added unto us, including health.

It makes no sense to pray for someone that has lung cancer from smoking and they go right back to smoking again. It makes no sense to pray for persons who are going to eat the same way and lacking exercise, without giving them the wisdom of Jesus Christ as being their Lord. They need to grow in the Word of God once healing has taken place.

- Bring them into the Kingdom of God,
- through salvation,
- through the sinner's prayer
- and then accepting Jesus Christ as their personal savior;
- Also introduce them to a change of heart and lifestyle that will maintain their deliverance and health.

In Matthew Jesus healed <u>all manner</u> of sickness and His fame grew. He healed those that were lunatic, and those possessed with demons.

- Matthew 4:24: There is no disease that Jesus cannot heal. The God we serve created this body and has the power to heal <u>all manner</u> of sickness and disease.
- You cannot lay hands on yourself or others if you do not believe God can heal. No matter the circumstances He is able to heal all manner of diseases.
- Torments: Jesus came to heal those that are tormented in their mind, emotionally, and physically. In

psychiatry, for instance there are all types of diseases. There are schizophrenia, bipolar, depression, personality issues, sleeping disorders, behavioral disorders, and dementia etc. However, the power of God is able to heal and deliver persons of every type of torments.
- Those that were possessed with devils: devils existed back then and they exist today. When it comes to sicknesses; the strategy is to discern if this thing is biological, neurological, self-inflicted through open doors, or the kind caused by those who are possessed.
- Go to your medical doctor; get checked to get proper assessment. As ministers of health and healing we do not want to be ignorant, we must operate in wisdom. Also, do not act without permission.

One of the things Jesus did was to lay hands. There is something powerful about laying hands on someone .The bible warns us not to lay hands on no man suddenly [1 Timothy 5:22]). It is the anointing and power of God in you flowing, do not forget that. Everything we see Jesus did in the Bible we should operate in. Remember that Jesus said greater works shall you do in my name.

- These are the signs that will follow them that believe in my name,
- They shall lay hands on the sick.

Jesus has transformed that anointing to the church–the called out ones.

1. To move in healing ministry you must have a personal relationship with Jesus Christ.
2. You must believe that Jesus is God, and that there is no disease that Jesus cannot heal.
3. Jesus has given this authority to the church.

The anointing resides in you. The Holy Spirit will teach you all things and you are anointed. It takes faith from all parties involved and the desire to be healed.

Chapter Reflections

1. _____
   _____
2. _____
   _____
3. _____
   _____

Segment Five

Access the Power

Chapter Twenty One

All These Shall Be Added

Many people do not know how to be great in the Kingdom of God. Just like the earthly Kingdom, there are certain things that make men great. However, the factors that make a man great differ greatly. In the earthly Kingdom, you can become great through dubious and unrighteous means.

As Kingdom citizens, there are benefits we can access through Christ. We need resources and materials to keep us focused on Kingdom things. When we were in the earthly and fleshly Kingdom, there are resources that make us identify with others in the Kingdom. We can talk about laws that govern the realm, and the things we can interact with, in the Kingdom.

However, in God's Kingdom, we need resources to channel our focus towards Heaven, so that the things of the world will not distract us. The Bible says,

> "Therefore we also, since we are surrounded by so great a cloud of witnesses, let us lay aside every weight, and the sin which so easily ensnares us, and let us run with endurance the race that is set before us, looking unto Jesus, the author and finisher of our faith, who for the joy that was set before Him endured the cross, despising the shame, and has sat down at the right hand of the throne of God." (Hebrews 12:1-2 NKJV)

While we journey through this path of faith, there are things we would do, and one of these, is to lay aside weights. There are certain things that are not sin, but they are weights. They hold us back from pressing into God. They hinder us from running the race that is set before us effectively. The issue is not always between the right and wrong choices, but sometimes, it is about things that hinder us from running the race set before us.

> "For assuredly, I say to you, till heaven and earth pass away, one jot or one tittle will by no means pass from the law till all is fulfilled. Whoever therefore breaks one of the least of these commandments, and teaches men so, shall be called least in the kingdom of heaven; but whoever does and teaches them, he shall be called great in the kingdom of heaven." (Matthew 5:18-19 NKJV)

We cannot tamper with the integrity of the Word of God, in that, everything in the law shall be fulfilled. The Word of God endures forever. The Word of God cannot fail. The Word of God cannot lie. While Jesus is not attempting to measure the gravity of the commandments in order to categorize them into least and great, He is bringing us to understand that we should not break any of the laws.

Anyone who practices and teaches the commandments of God is great in the Kingdom of Heaven. In God's Kingdom, greatness is not when you have wealth, riches, or valuable assets, but when you put God's commandments into action, and also encourage others to do so.

The Kingdom of Heaven is the place where Jesus lives. Jesus said that whosoever should teach the commandment of God would be exalted. Make it a duty to talk about Jesus at home, workplace, neighbourhood, anywhere you find yourself.

> "Assuredly, I say to you, among those born of women there has not risen one greater than John the Baptist; but he who is least in the kingdom of heaven is greater than he." (Matthew 11:11 NKJV)

John baptized Jesus. John was beheaded for preaching the Gospel and the King was upset. Jesus said that John was the greatest prophet. He was greater than all other prophets in the Old Testament were. Jesus said that if you come into the Kingdom of God, you would walk in the power of God. If you understand your authority in Christ, and as a Kingdom citizen, you are greater than John the Baptist was.

Your practice of God's Word, preaching the Kingdom and your encouragement to others is a way of evangelizing. When you do this, you become great! The definition of greatness differs from Kingdom to Kingdom. The Lord also said that the ones who is the chief servant is the greatest in the Kingdom (Matthew 23:11).

Many will never have an opportunity to preach in front of the multitudes. The Lord might just give you 10 congregants and you will be great in the Kingdom. It is not by numbers, but your obedience to do God's will. It is not about the Word of God that you know, but the Word of God that you practice and teach others.

If you are in God's Kingdom, you are going to have all. The Bible says;

> "And my God shall supply all your need according to His riches in glory by Christ Jesus." (Philippians 4:19 NKJV)

Do not compare yourself with anyone on social media or any other platforms. Be grateful, for whatever you have, wherever you find yourself, and ensure that you are aligned with God's Word. God supplies our needs,

> *It is not by numbers, but your obedience to do God's will*

and He supplies, not according to our riches, but according to His riches. The Lord loves humility. You should ensure that the things you see, do not drive you.

Some people put everything they do on social media in order to receive validation from people. They are trying to receive greatness from others. You cannot receive greatness from man; greatness comes from God. Friendship with the world is enmity against God. You cannot be a friend of the world and at the same time be a friend with God.

You cannot be great by posting everything going on about your life on social media. If you try to make a man love you, you are exalting yourself and God will bring you low.

> "At that time the disciples came to Jesus, saying, "Who then is greatest in the kingdom of heaven?" Then Jesus called a little child to Him, set him in the midst of them, and said, "Assuredly, I say to you, unless you are converted and become as little children, you will by no means enter the kingdom of heaven. Therefore whoever humbles himself as this little child is the greatest in the kingdom of heaven. Whoever receives one little child like this in My name receives Me." (Matthew 18; 1-5 NKJV)

Jesus hates pride. Pride goes before a fall. Destruction follows pride. The Bible says,

> "Pride goes before destruction, and a haughty spirit before a fall." (Proverbs 16:18 NKJV)

> "When pride comes, then comes shame; but with the humble is wisdom." (Proverbs 11:2 NKJV)

> "A man's pride will bring him low, but the humble in spirit will retain honor." (Proverbs 29:23 NKJV)

God created all of us; He hates pride. God hates spiritual pride. He hates it when people pretend or parade themselves around. Jesus said, "Unless you humble yourself, you would not be great." Lower yourself before the Lord. Acknowledge Him. We are in trouble, if we do not pray and humble ourselves before the Lord. I am not pleased when pastors say, "My church." It is God's Church. You did not die for the Church, Christ did. Humble yourself.

> "But you, do not be called 'Rabbi'; for One is your Teacher, the Christ, and you are all brethren. Do not call anyone on earth your father; for One is your Father, He who is in heaven. And do not be called teachers; for One is your Teacher, the Christ. But he who is greatest among you

> shall be your servant. And whoever exalts himself will be humbled, and he who humbles himself will be exalted." (Matthew 23:10-11 NKJV)

If your work organization or any other asks you to do something illegal, you must say no. If you make Jesus your Master, then He must direct you every day. You must look unto Jesus, the author and finisher of your faith. Man is not your source, Jesus is. The Lord can bless you in millions of ways. If you look at man, man will fail you. The Lord provides, and He uses people as a channel.

> "But seek first the kingdom of God and His righteousness, and all these things shall be added to you." (Matthew 6:33 NKJV)

The Kingdom of God is our priority. When we seek God's Kingdom and righteousness, we come into the abundance of our needs. Giving us our desires is not God's problem, but our priority. Many times, we leave the Kingdom of God, and run after the things that should be added to us. God does not want anything to take His place in our lives, so He guards our priority.

Jesus is saying that if you seek that which is spiritual (The Kingdom), even the things that are physical (these things) shall be added to you. Are you seeking prosperity? Your heart should not be set upon riches, but on the Kingdom of God. Our disposition should be to love God unconditionally and do His will, and we will see that even God takes care of our needs. The Bible says,

> "Therefore, I say to you, do not worry about your life, what you will eat or what you will drink; nor about your body, what you will put on. Is not life more than food and the body more than clothing? Look at the birds of the air, for they neither sow nor reap nor gather into barns; yet your heavenly Father feeds them. Are you not of more value than they? Which of you by worrying can add one cubit to his stature? "So why do you worry about clothing? Consider the lilies of the field, how they grow: they neither toil nor spin; and yet I say to you that even Solomon in all his glory was not arrayed like one of these. Now, if God so clothes the grass of the field, which today is, and tomorrow is thrown into the oven, will He not much more clothe you, O you of little faith? "Therefore do not worry, saying, 'What shall we eat?' or 'What shall we drink?' Or 'What shall we wear?' For after all these things the Gentiles seek. For your heavenly Father knows that you need all these things. But seek first the kingdom of God and His righteousness, and all these things shall be added to you". (Matthew 6:25-33 NKJV)

Our Heavenly Father knows our needs. He knows the things we need. We should ensure that our hearts are set upon the things above, so that God can look below to grant us the provision to our needs.

Chapter Reflections

1. _____

_____

2. _____

_____

3. _____

_____

Chapter Twenty Two

The Prayer Of God

The Bible establishes that the Kingdom of God is a real place filled with authority and power. It is a set apart confinement for God and his supernatural beings. The birth of Jesus on Earth (who is a member of the trinity) is an expansion of the Kingdom of heaven on Earth. The mandate given to us, as humans, from God, is to ensure that we live the fulfilment of our lives in Christ.

A practical example of this is the study of the life of Jesus; who spent his existence on Earth fulfilling the course of his father who had sent him to do the job. We can only live a life that conforms to the fulfilment of heaven on Earth by building a life of prayer. Jesus Christ taught His disciples about prayer, by demonstration, and the template we call 'The Lord's Prayer.' It is rather a prayer pattern the believers (His disciples) and not the Lord's Prayer.

What is prayer?

Prayer is like an aroma that goes before the Lord. Nothing changes without the earnest act of prayer. Prayer is how we communicate with God; making our request known to him, praising him and hearing from him. As Christians, prayer has proven to be a necessity for survival. Prayer needs specific requirements and one of these requirements was established in Jeremiah 33:3 – "Call unto me and I'll answer thee, and shew thee great and mighty things which thou knowest not." If we worship the Lord in Spirit and in truth and believe (what we pray is done) when we prayer, there is no doubt that our prayer will be answered.

The tremendous power in prayer cannot be overemphasized. Prayer is effective in the following ways:

1. Prayer unlocks the heaven
2. Prayer transports men into the eternity of time.
3. Prayer is like a deposit into a bank account, with time; it releases blessings.
4. When prayer is released, power is generated.

In the course of prayer, the Holy Spirit is the partner that helps us to access the wisdom of heaven through prayers and He helps us to pray the will of the father (God). It is interesting to know that God has his own prayer request.

> "In this manner, therefore, pray: Our Father in heaven, Hallowed be Your name. Your will be done on earth as it is heaven. Give us this day our daily bread. And forgive us our debts, as we forgive our debtors. And do not lead us into temptation, but deliver us from the evil one. For yours is the kingdom and the power and the glory forever. Amen." (Matt 6:9-13 NKJV)

In prayer, you must understand that the authority and power to the answers to your prayers is not coming from you but from heaven. The first thing to do in prayer is to acknowledge Our father and the Kingdom of heaven which has given us the access to pray. It is God's desire that we call Him Father. We are His children; we have the spirit of adoption with which we call Abba Father. This is our confidence, that when we call upon our Father, He will answer us. So that we will not assume that we talk to an earthly father, Jesus said, "Our Father in heaven". We do not pray to our father in the earth, but our Father in heaven. Prayer is meant to start with an acknowledgment of the Father. He is the recipient of our prayers. Praise helps us to regard and honour the father to whom our prayer is directed.

In the Old Testament, the people saw God as great, holy and righteous being who is far away beyond their reach. An attempt to relate with God as a Father seems like

> *This is our confidence, that when we call upon our Father, He will answer us.*

impossible. Jesus, who came as the mediator, created prayer as bridge to connect and restore us to the Father. He is not far away. We are to approach the Father as a son or daughter. Jesus said, "Our Father", and not "My father". The Spirit of God in us made us qualified to call God our Father.

God wants His will to be done on Earth as it is in heaven. This is God's prayer request which He wants us to declare. Your prayers as a Christian should be cantered on the will of the Kingdom of God being manifested in the earth. Your prayer should be directed towards fulfilling the will of God upon the earth. The will of God is being done in heaven. However, God brought man to the earth for him to exercise dominion towards establishing the will of God in every sphere of influence.

It is the will of God that He provides our daily bread. He is Jehovah Jireh; He provides for the needs of His people. To shed some light when the Hebrew people mentioned bread they meant everything. They were not just talking about food. Their bread is everything that they need to be sustained in life (money, favour, clothes, shelter, health etc.). He is glorified when we have needs met. We must set adequate time apart to pray.

Ensure that there is nothing in your life, home or heart that would give the enemy a right to block you from receiving from your heavenly father. An unforgiving spirit, for example, hinders the efficacy of prayer in a man's life. Prayer is effective when we forgive others. God also forgive sin. Therefore, we must learn to confess our sins, and ask for the forgiveness through the blood of the Christ.

> *Prayer is effective when we forgive others.*

Prayer also helps us to get God's leading. God can helps us to not to fall into temptation. With His leading, we will not fall into traps were we are weak and will fall from his grace. In other words, prayer helps us to get direction to live our lives, from falling into the hands of the evil one. We must know that the Kingdom belongs to the Lord, the power and the Glory, and it will be forever.

Conclusively, prayer is the only channel to the power and authority of the Kingdom. Therefore, this model of prayer can transform our life. We should learn to pray like Jesus, so that we can experience God's hand in everything we do.

Chapter Twenty Three

Carrying The Fire And The Healing

The Creator created no one with a sickness or any disease, even if anyone was born with a sickness, it cannot be traced to the Creator, and there must have been other factors responsible for that. Every now and then, diseases cease the existence of people. People now die of cancer, infections, cardiovascular diseases, mental illnesses; amongst others. If Jesus were to be on earth in this present age, what would he have done? To answer that, we must consider what He did when He existed as a man on earth. Were there sick people when Jesus was walking on the surface of the earth? Yes they were. What did Jesus do to them, He healed as many who had contact with Him. Even in some cases, He only needed to speak from where He was, and the one's sick were healed at that same hour.

In Luke 4:16-20, Jesus read from the book of Prophet Isaiah; "The Spirit of the LORD is upon me, because He has anointed me to preach the Gospel to the poor. He has sent me to heal the brokenhearted, to preach deliverance to the captives and recovery of sight to the blind, to set at liberty those who are being oppressed,"(Vs 18). Since this prophecy is about Jesus, then, as part of Jesus' Kingdom, we also carry the same mandate to heal the sick, and deliver the oppressed. In order to be effective in the healing ministry, there is need for us to first identify the need for healing.

The fall of Man

Man was always in deep fellowship with God, he was able to relate with God very closely since he was the reflection of God. The Glory of God was so heavy upon man, and it made every other creatures to see him as the representation of God. Adam and Eve were placed in the garden planted by God; Eden. Eden can be translated to mean; "the presence of God". As long as man was doing according to that which the Lord had said, man was at peace with God. When man sinned suddenly, the unexpected happened. The Glory that had always been covering them departed. God declared His judgement over the serpent, the man and the woman. The element of stress and pain can be traced out from God's judgement. This was because man became spiritually dead. The truth is, when a person becomes spiritually dead, the fellow is exposed to any form of attack in all aspects of life. So, it is not untrue to say that sin is the source of all forms of sicknesses and diseases.

The bacteria and fungi were created by God not so that they could harm men (Colossians 1:16). They are to aid the existence of men, hence, with the fall of man, various manipulations have taken place in the space, and these things that ought to aid the existence of man now have side effects of mankind.

In Exodus 15:26, Moses talking to the people of Israel said; "If you diligently heed the voice of the LORD your God and do what is right in His sight, give ear to His commandments and keep all His statutes, I will put none of the diseases on you which I have brought on the Egyptians". The emphasis here is on the act of obedience. Since it was disobedience to God's command that led to the fall of man. Obedience became an essential commodity to keep man in tune with God.

Idolatry

God, as the Creator of the universe, does not share His Glory with anyone or anything. When a creature begin to ascribe the glory of creation and supremacy to another creature, it brings a whole lot of negative effects. The disobedience of man in Eden did not end in Eden, but has continued up till now. Men now ascribe the supreme glory to images, which they sacrifice to as idols and even refer to as their god. This dumb act is another thing that brings sickness on mankind.

Exodus 23:25, God talking to the tribe of Israel through Moses, "So you shall serve the LORD your God, and He will bless your bread and your water. And I will take sickness away from the midst of you". The 24th verse of that same scripture actually begins with; "You shall not bow down to their gods nor serve them".

The sin of idolatry can be very detrimental to the lives of mankind. What God expects from us is to reference Him and give Him the glory and honor that He deserves. One of the effects of giving His glory to idols and images is the exposure to sicknesses and diseases.

There are thousands of diseases that had been identified to be existing in the medical world (under 39 classifications). However, sicknesses can manifest in the following organs and systems in the human body.

- From the head to the toe
- Outside skin diseases(skin disorders)
- Mental diseases(illnesses)
- Cardiovascular systems
- Lungs system
- Endocrine system
- Reproductive system
- Muscle, Bone, and Joint systems

The skin, being the largest organ in the body, is exposed to various hazards every now and then.

The good news is, no matter how serious a health condition is, God is willing to heal His people. Obviously, a sick man is not a happy man. God wants His creatures to duly serve and worship Him, and for us to be able to do this effectively as human-beings, there is a need for us to be in good and sound health. God is not delighted to see us in pains, He is not willing to keep us in our challenges; as that does not give Him pleasure. What gives God pleasure is the sanity of His people.

So, if anyone is sick, God is always willing to have them healed. It is God's utmost delight to see an insane man regaining His sanity. God is delighted whenever He sees an oppressed woman rising from her state of sickness. When sicknesses depart from men, the Glory is given to God, hence, it gladdens the heart of God, when the Glory that is due to His Holy Name, is given to Him.

"God talking to the people of Israel through Moses, "And the Lord will take away from you all sickness, and will afflict you with none of the terrible diseases of Egypt which you have known, but will lay them on all those who hate you." Deuteronomy 7:15

God is not delighted to see us in pains.

Notice that God was not willing to heal just a few of the sicknesses, not some, not most, not many, but ALL.

No matter the condition, no matter what the situation might be, God is willing to heal.

Sometimes, doctors would have given their verdict; they would have concluded about a health challenge and even give their patient a time frame that the fellow might have to live. Over and over again, the miracle working power of God had been seen at work in lives. Men who have been condemned to die, have risen up from their state of hopelessness into sound health. Certain people even died of sicknesses, but they came back to life again, without any sickness in their body. It is not in God's agenda to have you on that sick bed forever. It is not His will to keep you in that sick posture for the rest of your life. God would not be delighted to watch you die on that sick bed, He is so interested in getting you out of your physical, or mental oppression. God is not unaware of the fact that you really need to be physically fit for you to also be spiritually sound and alert.

Every sick person needs a healing, and every healing comes from a healer. The process of healing is not limited to a dimension. God being the Healer, can decide to perform the healing in diverse ways. It is quite unlikely that God would come down by Himself to perform the healing works when there are men on earth who can carry that out on His behalf. If God is going to heal the sick, believers must make themselves so aligned with His word. They must become His channels in reaching out to others. The healing power is not that which God cannot give to men that love and fear Him. Hence, He had already given this power to as many as they believe in Him. For as many as they that believe in Him, to them He gave power to become sons of God (John 1:12). If then we are truly His sons, then, we have the capacity to do that which God is able to do.

Jesus speaking in Mark 16:17-18, "And these signs will follow those who believe; in My name they will cast out demons...they will lay hands on the sick, and they will recover".

Jesus was saying to His disciples and by extension, every believer that believes in His Holy Name have signs that will follow them, and one of those signs is the capacity to heal the sick. The question is; why do we have believers who seem not to have this kind of ability to heal? The truth is, as much as many of us believe in the name of Jesus, our belief is only in existence verbally; our faith is shaken when it comes to practicing our confession. In other words, believers are not able to express their healing ability simply because they don't believe. Jesus simply made it clear that as long as anyone believes in His Name, such individual will be able to heal this sick. So, many times, it is never the Name of Jesus that is ineffective, it is our faith that is weak

> *Believers are not able to express their healing ability simply because they don't believe.*

or little; it's not even as big as a mustard seed, for if it were, it would be able to move a mountain.

To be effective in the healing works of Christ, a quick look at the following;

- Believe in the name of Jesus.

- Pray for the sick using the Name of Jesus.

- Call the sickness or diseases by name as you command it to leave in the Name of Jesus Christ.

- Give yourself to the study of God's Word, for us to be equipped to know and understand the perfect will of God for His people.

- Commune with God constantly in the place of prayer.

- Be passionately committed to evangelism, as the healing sign follow on those that are on the move.

If you are sick, receive your healing now in Jesus Name! If anyone is sick around you, there is a mandate on you to heal them. May your faith be strengthened! May you be able to walk in God's dimensions of healing, by the fire of the Lord! Amen.

Chapter Reflections

1. _____
_____

2. _____
_____

3. _____
_____

Chapter Twenty Four

10 Powerful Prayers To Bring Victory In Your Life

How to Overcome the Strong man

Then a blind and dumb man under the power of a demon was brought to Jesus, and He cured him, so that the blind and dumb man both spoke and saw. And all the [crowds of] people were stunned with bewildered wonder and said, This cannot be the Son of David, can it? But the Pharisees, hearing it, said, This Man drives out demons only by and with the help of Beelzebub, the prince of demons. And knowing their thoughts, He said to them, Any kingdom that is divided against itself is being brought to desolation and laid waste, and no city or house divided against itself will last or continue to stand. And if Satan drives out Satan, he has become divided against himself and disunified; how then will his kingdom last or continue to stand? And if I drive out the demons by [help of] Beelzebub, by whose [help] do your sons drive them out? For this reason they shall be your judges. But if it is by the Spirit of God that I drive out the demons, then the kingdom of God has come upon you [before you expected it]. Or how can a person go into a strong man's house and carry off his goods (the entire equipment of his house) without first binding the strong man? Then indeed he may plunder his house (Matthew 12:22-29 AMP).

Jesus' ministry entailed salvation, healing and deliverance. The devil has a demonic system and he has many princes (that rules with rulers of darkness, powers and spiritual wickedness in high places) that have been established against one's life. This oppression causes violation against God's word.

Only it must be in faith that he asks with no wavering (no hesitating, no doubting). For the one who wavers (hesitates, doubts) is like the billowing surge out at sea that is blown hither and thither and tossed by the wind. For truly, let not such a person imagine that he will receive anything [he asks for] from the Lord, [For being as he is] a man of two minds (hesitating, dubious, irresolute), [he is] unstable and unreliable and uncertain about everything [he thinks, feels, decides] (James 1:6-8 AMP).

We need to keep a right relationship with God and those around us. The greatest warfare is keeping everything in unity in the spirit. Unity in the family, among the churches; putting aside denominations, views, ideologies and doctrines and allowing Jesus to be the center and core, we will see the mighty move of God in our lives and the world– at large. Going against the will of God puts us in warfare. If we don't put our lives, families and spirit in order; getting the vision of God for our lives we will not move forward.

Remember, we don't pray for demons, they need to be bound and cast out. They must be driven out of peoples' lives, household and the invisible world. Jesus says in Matthew 18:18 '...whatever you bound on earth shall be bound in Heaven...'

> Truly I tell you, whatever you forbid and declare to be improper and unlawful on earth must be what is already forbidden in heaven, and whatever you permit and declare proper and lawful on earth must be what is already permitted in heaven (Matthew 18:18 AMP).

We need to use the weapons of our warfare which are the blood of Jesus, the name of Jesus and the authority we have by sitting in heavenly places to gain victory.

> Put on God's whole armor [the armor of a heavy-armed soldier which God supplies], that you may be able successfully to stand up against [all] the strategies and the deceits of the devil. For we are not wrestling with flesh and blood [contending only with physical opponents], but against the despotisms, against the powers against [the master spirits who are] the world rulers of this present darkness, against the spirit forces of wickedness in the heavenly (supernatural) sphere. Therefore put on God's complete armor, that you may be able to resist and stand your ground on the evil day [of danger], and having done all [the crisis demands], to stand [firmly in your place] (Ephesians 6: 11-13).

If you want the deep things of God; solutions to deep problems, we need to make serious prayers in the Spirit by the Holy Spirit. The Kingdom of God is demonstrated when it brings salvation, healing and deliverance to people's lives

The Kingdom of God is stronger than any other kingdom.

> But if it is by the Spirit of God that I drive out the demons, then the Kingdom of God has come upon you [before you expected it] (Matthew 12:28 AMP).

> When the strong man, fully armed, [from his courtyard] guards his own dwelling, his belongings are undisturbed [his property is at peace and is secure] But when one stronger than he attacks him and conquers him, he robs him of his whole armor on which he had relied and divides up and distributes all his goods as plunder (spoil) (Luke 11:21 AMP).

In the battle of life, it is either an individual is strong or the strong man is stronger which will enable him to take over the individual's life. The way to get strength is through prayers.

> In conclusion, be strong in the Lord [be empowered through your union with Him]; draw your strength from Him [that strength which His boundless might provides] (Ephesians 6:10 AMP).

If an individual is going to break through, he/she must learn how to bind, cancel and rebuke through the Spirit of God, with the name of Jesus and the blood of Jesus.

The strong man in an individual's life can be poverty, lack, addiction, propensity to a certain sin. Prayer reveals the strong man. Sin opens the door for the strong man to come in. Fear, un-forgiveness and certain evil covenants give the devil a legal ground to operate. We need to know our rights and authority in heavenly places. We need to apply the blood of Jesus heavily against the strong man on everything that pertains to us. The blood of Jesus breaks demonic covenants and contracts, and empowers. The power of God is able to go into our past and undo every finished work of darkness and into the future to pave ways.

Some problems are caused by strange powers resisting the move and manifestation of God in an individual's life. In Luke 11:24 the enemy understands that the body is the house of an individual. The enemy (unclean spirits) has occupied various parts of an individual's body to torment such individual. This enemy prevents individuals from living above sin or subjecting their bodies to the Word of God. He wants an individual and generations to be put to destruction via sickness, bondage, defeat, and other negative means.

When we get our deliverance from sin and the works of the devil, we need to maintain and guard our deliverance. Deliverance without salvation and a prayer life is nothing. We need to bind the strong man, cancel generational curses, forces of hell, and every work of darkness daily and fill our lives with prayer and the Word of God. We need to limit the time we spend wasting time, seeing the television and spend much time fortifying our lives and everything that pertains to us. Most of our problems get deep roots because of our negative thinking patterns and actions. The devil gives us all the negative things we think in our hearts. We need to deal with negative thoughts.

> And when it arrives, it finds [the place] swept and put in order and furnished and decorated (Luke 11:25 AMP).

Our problems seems to reoccur severally because when the enemy was cast out, it came back refortified with several (seven) other demons. This is one of the reasons we need to stay close to Jesus because we cannot defeat the strong man on our own. The enemy we don't defeat through prayers and the Word of God will defeat and destroy our lives completely.

The war is not centered on us but centered on the Kingdom of Jesus Christ and the Kingdom of Satan. We have an opportunity in life to choose which army we are going to stand for; the army of God or the devil's army. If we are on the Lord's army, the devil becomes furious and tries every possible means to attack our lives, assignment and destiny. The greater the glory and assignment of God on an individual, the greater the battle he/she is likely to face in life but there is good news. In Revelations 12:7 and 8 ...Michael prevailed... the angels of the Lord will always prevail over the strong man.

> Then I heard a strong (loud) voice in heaven, saying, Now it has come—the salvation and the power and the kingdom (the dominion, the reign) of our God, and the power (the sovereignty, the authority) of His Christ (the Messiah); for the accuser of our brethren, he who keeps bringing before our God charges against them day and night, has been cast out! And they have overcome (conquered) him by means of the blood of the Lamb and by the utterance of their testimony, for they did not love and cling to life even when faced with death [holding their lives cheap till they had to die for their witnessing] (Revelations 12:10 and 11 AMP).

Victory is ascertained in Jesus Christ if only we can believe in the finished work of Christ and pray relentlessly.

Prayers

- Let the blood of Jesus go into my past a thousand generation from my mother and father sides. I ask the Lord through the power and mercy of the Lord Jesus Christ by the Holy Spirit and the authority that is in the blood of Jesus Christ. I pray that the powerful blood of Jesus will break every covenant and bring deliverance to every curse that gave the strong man access to my life and generation, dry up and die in the name of Jesus Christ.

- I decree according to Revelations 12:10 that salvation and strength is come to overcome the strong man in the name of Jesus Christ.
- I declare the Kingdom of God comes now to override the strong man in my life in the name of Jesus Christ.
- Revelations 12:10 I declare the power of the anointed One Christ Jesus and the blood of Jesus destroy the strong man in my life in the name of Jesus Christ.
- I declare the power of Christ and the blood of Jesus destroy the strong man of accusation in my life in Jesus' name.
- I declare that through the blood of Jesus you unravel the strong man's assignment for my life in the name of Jesus Christ.
- I declare right now that through the blood of Jesus every ancestral tie to the strong man against my life dry up and die now in the name of Jesus Christ.
- Every place that the strong man has occupied and taken residence in my life I command you to be uprooted from my marital life, finances, career, emotions and die in the name of Jesus Christ.
- I command the strong man to pack whatever tools he has left in my life. You are being evicted out of my body, spirit, soul, family and marriage. Your eviction is being served in the name of Jesus Christ.

- I release now the sanctifying blood of Jesus to wash out where the strong man has lived in my life in the name of Jesus Christ.
- I declare that every strong man operating in the heavens with every heavenly being and powers working against my life be disconnected and driven to the pit of hell in the name of Jesus Christ.
- I decree that every backlash of the enemy over my life is defeated by the blood of Jesus Christ. I declare victory over every strong man in the name of Jesus Christ.

Chapter Reflections

1. _____

2. _____

3. _____

You are now empowered with the Power of God!

More Books By
Dr. Kelafo And Shallaywa Collie

Go Global Leadership Keys: Strategies for Your Business, Brand and Organization to Have Global Impact You are my Father; I am your Son - Understanding Kingdom Sonship (Revised)

A Lifetime Relationship: Life Building Time in the Presence of God, 52 Week Devotional for Men and Women

Victory: 21 Powerful, Prayerful Biblical Declarations to Begin Your Day

Heavenly Prayers to Live Inspired, Empowered and Fulfilled Daily (Revised)

Practical Keys to Knowing Christ to Walk In Deliverance, Purpose and Destiny (Revised)

The Kingdom: Experience Heaven on Earth

The Kingdom: Experience Heaven on Earth Part II

Available on www.Amazon.com

For more materials, to connect with and book Dr. Kelafo and Shallaywa Collie, visit and subscribe to these platforms:

www.kamgbahamas.com

www.kelafoczcollie.com

www.shallaywa.com

www.majesticpriesthoodpublications.com

YouTube: Kami Bahamas

www.ingramcontent.com/pod-product-compliance
Lightning Source LLC
LaVergne TN
LVHW051541070426
835507LV00021B/2357